G000045117

Researching PRiMARY EDUCATiON

SAGE was founded in 1965 by Sara Miller McCune to support the dissemination of usable knowledge by publishing innovative and high-quality research and teaching content. Today, we publish over 900 journals, including those of more than 400 learned societies, more than 800 new books per year, and a growing range of library products including archives, data, case studies, reports, and video. SAGE remains majority-owned by our founder, and after Sara's lifetime will become owned by a charitable trust that secures our continued independence.

Los Angeles | London | New Delhi | Singapore | Washington DC | Melbourne

Researching
PRIMARY
EDUCATION

Edited by

REBECCA AUSTIN

Los Angeles | London | New Delhi
Singapore | Washington DC | Melbourne

Learning Matters
An imprint of SAGE Publications Ltd
1 Oliver's Yard
55 City Road
London EC1Y 1SP

SAGE Publications Inc.
2455 Teller Road
Thousand Oaks, California 91320

SAGE Publications India Pvt Ltd
B 1/I 1 Mohan Cooperative Industrial Area
Mathura Road
New Delhi 110 044

SAGE Publications Asia-Pacific Pte Ltd
3 Church Street
#10–04 Samsung Hub
Singapore 049483

Editor: Amy Thornton
Development Editor: Jennifer Clark
Production Controller: Chris Marke
Project Management: Deer Park Productions
Marketing Manager: Lorna Patkai
Cover Design: Wendy Scott
Typeset by: C&M Digitals (P) Ltd, Chennai, India
Printed and bound by CPI Group (UK) Ltd,
Croydon, CR0 4YY

© Rebecca Austin, Wendy Cobb, Judy Durrant,
Gill Hope, Kristy Howells, Peter Gregory
and Viv Wilson

First published by Learning Matters/ SAGE 2016

Apart from any fair dealing for the purposes of
research or private study, or criticism or review, as
permitted under the Copyright, Design and Patents
Act, 1988, this publication may be reproduced,
stored or transmitted in any form, or by any
means, only with the prior permission in writing
of the publishers, or in the case of reprographic
reproduction, in accordance with the terms of
licences issued by the Copyright Licensing Agency.
Enquiries concerning reproduction outside these
terms should be sent to the publishers.

Library of Congress Control Number: 2016930686

British Library Cataloguing in Publication Data

A catalogue record for this book is available from the
British Library.

ISBN 978-1-4739-4813-6 (pbk)
ISBN 978-1-4739-4812-9

At SAGE we take sustainability seriously. Most of our products are printed in the UK using FSC papers and boards.
When we print overseas we ensure sustainable papers are used as measured by the PREPS grading system.
We undertake an annual audit to monitor our sustainability.

Contents

About the authors

Dr Rebecca Austin teaches on the Primary English courses across a range of initial teacher education, masters and doctoral programmes in the Faculty of Education at Canterbury Christ Church University. She has a lead role in developing research in the faculty around the theme of 'Pedagogy and Identity'. Her current research interests are concerned with newly qualified teachers and literacy co-ordinators beliefs about the teaching of Primary English in schools. She is also involved in a project to develop academic writing with undergraduate student teachers.

Wendy Cobb is a Senior Lecturer in the Faculty of Education at Canterbury Christ Church University where she teaches on a number of initial teacher education pathways. She is project lead for a partnership initiative which focuses on leadership for social and emotional learning. Wendy is also professional studies lead and research supervisor for a PGCE programme at a School Centred Initial Teaching Training Partnership. In addition, she works as an independent education consultant with a particular interest in Primary Languages.

Dr Judy Durrant is a Principal Lecturer in the Faculty of Education at Canterbury Christ Church University. She is involved in a range of postgraduate teaching, leadership and development, with particular interest in teacher leadership, professional agency and identity, organisational development and practitioner research. She supports research and development groups for cross-faculty multi-professional working and social and emotional learning as well as school-based action research projects and funded evaluations, including recent consultancy in Palestine and the Philippines. She leads professional development for teacher educators. Her PhD thesis focused on the role of teachers in school change, using a portraiture methodology.

Dr Peter Gregory has taught across all phases of education across the South East. In schools he has led subject development and curriculum design as well as undertaking local authority advisory work. He is currently Principal Lecturer in Education at Canterbury Christ Church University and regularly teaches and presents research across the UK, Europe and beyond. In his role as Faculty Director of Partner-led Action and Research Development he works with groups of teachers and other professionals to inspire their investigations. Peter is President Elect of the National Society for Education in Art and Design (NSEAD) and a World Councillor for the

International Society for Education through Art (InSEA). He also chairs the Expert Subject Advisory Group (ESAG) which was originally set up by DfE to advise schools on the implementation of the national curriculum.

Dr Gill Hope is a recently retired senior lecturer from the Faculty of Education at Canterbury Christ Church University. During her years there, she taught research methodology to students on the Primary Education Progression Route (with QTS), a level 6 course for students with a Foundation Degree. She also worked with students at Master's level and is continuing to support doctoral students on both EdD and PhD pathways. Her specialism is Design & Technology Education but her interests include creativity and the development of human cognition.

Dr Kristy Howells is the Faculty of Education Director of Physical Education at Canterbury Christ Church University. She teaches across a range of undergraduate and postgraduate degree programmes and ITE provision that include Physical Education and Physical Activity. She is particularly passionate about Physical Education and Physical Activity and these are the areas of her research. She has disseminated her findings to schools, through book chapters and national and international conferences.

Dr Viv Wilson is an experienced teacher educator with over 30 years' experience. Much of her work involves supporting students' research investigations at undergraduate and post-graduate levels, including helping to develop their academic writing. She was awarded a National Teaching Fellowship in 2014.

Chapter 1

Introduction

Rebecca Austin

Objectives

This chapter:

- sets out the aims of the book;
- contextualises the notion of research in primary education;
- outlines the content, purpose and key features of each chapter.

Introduction

We eat a lot of popcorn in my house and I realised recently that it would probably be cheaper, easier and more fun to cut out the middle man and pop the corn ourselves. There are a very wide variety of popcorn makers to choose from online and I spent some time looking at the technical specifications, the style, colour, size and so on. Some came with extra freebies, so I tried to work out which of these offers was good value and which was not. I sorted the list of popcorn makers by price (low to high) and by popularity (high to low) and looked for ones which were in the top ten of both lists. I realised that 'oil free' and 'healthy' were variations on the same selling point. I read the customer reviews – good and bad – and considered the reasonableness of the criticism and the balance of the praise. I looked at the average star ratings and hesitated over those with five stars from the one and only customer who had reviewed their purchase. I finally placed my order for the popcorn maker which seemed to me to best fit what I wanted, at a price that suited me, that I believed would do the job well and one with a look that l liked. In effect, I undertook purposeful, systematic research.

Similarly, research in teaching is, at its heart, simply a more disciplined and structured version of the kind of research described above that all of us have done countless times in our daily lives. We start with something we want to find out; we collect, sort and critique information about it and then we reach a conclusion. You might have thought me strange if I'd randomly selected a popcorn maker from the given list – extravagant if I had simply bought the most expensive assuming that it would be the best; foolish if I had bought the one that had that one five star review from someone I didn't know. In your work in primary schools you will be putting into practice a whole range of ideas and approaches that come from a wide range of sources and part of your role is to make choices about how you teach by finding out what works in your classroom and what doesn't and why. Research is the vehicle through which you do this.

This book will take you through the process of designing, implementing and writing up small-scale research projects undertaken as a practitioner-researcher in primary schools so that you and the children you teach can benefit in specific ways from your time together in (and out of) the classroom.

Purposeful, systematic research in the primary school classroom is the means by which practitioners can make informed decisions about the best ways to engage in teaching and learning in the classroom so that they can justify their practice and enhance the learning of the children with whom they work.

What makes primary schools unique?

Unlike the usual secondary model of education, a full-time primary teacher is likely to teach a whole class of children for the majority of their lessons every day for the majority of the school year. They are the key adult in the classroom providing pastoral support and care alongside their teaching role and they are likely to have knowledge of the child outside of the classroom through their interactions with parents, carers and the wider community. As a teacher in a primary school classroom you can build significant, professional and personal relationships with the children with whom you work – getting to know them really well as individual learners in different circumstances within the school day. Primary practitioners, over time, are therefore able to build relationships of trust within a 'community of practice' (Lave and Wenger, 1991) where they can establish how learning works in their classroom for the children with whom they work.

In addition, learning in primary schools can be examined not only in the context of individual subjects but also across subjects and even outside of timetabled learning slots – in the playground and beyond. Children's learning behaviours and attitudes can be the focus for research and the ways in which children learn best in the different situations in which they find themselves can be investigated. Furthermore, primary school contexts give access to a reasonably sized yet contained sample from which research participants can be recruited. Primary schools, large or small, provide opportunities to look at learning and development across years and key stages; teachers and teaching assistants who are already part of the learning community are easily accessible, and existing links with families and the wider community can support the development of research outside the school environment.

The microcosm of the primary classroom or school as a multipurpose learning environment presents the aspiring researcher with a wealth of investigative possibilities from which to choose.

Why should I research?

Chapter 2 develops the idea of primary teachers as researchers and considers the role of different kinds of research and research findings which are used in developing 'research informed practice'. It explores the reasons why teachers should see themselves as researchers, and how research by teachers and by others can be used to underpin teaching and learning in the classroom. Lingard and Renshaw (2010, p27) argue for a 'researcherly disposition' for all teachers – those who are creators, users and objects of research and understand its significance in developing practice.

Some of you reading this book will be reading it because you are required to undertake a formal research project or investigation as part of the assessed work on an education course you are following. You might not have chosen to research – and therefore might not even have considered researching at all without the promise of a qualification as the motivation. Others of you will already be sold on the idea that research is an essential aspect of your role as a teacher – you might have opted for further study for the very reason that it will provide you with the opportunity to undertake research. The fact that most, if not all, initial teacher education courses include an assessed research project as part of the training programme suggests that it is seen as an integral part of being a teacher. One of the aims of this book is to present the idea of research to you in a very broad sense as well as guiding you through the narrower requirements of an assessed piece. In its broadest sense, research is about getting better at teaching by looking closely at what happens in the classroom or considering new or other ways of doing it. This is not an unreasonable expectation of teachers – knowing why you do what you do is at the core of being a professional and you need to have informed arguments to support your approaches, otherwise you might just as well buy the first popcorn maker on the list!

A research-based approach to developing your practice provides you with evidence to effect change in your teaching, your classroom, your school, yourself and beyond.

Where do I begin?

The kind of research that this book is most concerned with is that which takes place on a small scale, in a classroom or school and which enables the teacher as researcher to find out *something* about *anything* that takes place within the context of the children's primary education experience. One way of thinking about research in education is as a huge bubbling pot of stew. Each piece of research adds something to the mix, to the flavour of what is perceived or understood about education and all that it encompasses. The kind of classroom investigations or research in which you are most likely to engage will probably add the equivalent of one sliver of carrot or a grain of salt to that stew – but everything adds to the mix – reinforcing what is already there or adding a complementary or contrasting flavour.

Chapter 3 helps you think about the very beginnings of research – how to frame your interest as a question so that you can set about finding some answers. It will guide you through the process of exploring ideas for research and narrowing your focus so that you can look in detail at a very particular element of your area of interest. It is essential that the question you ask is expressed in such a way that you know what information you will need to be able to answer it (and the importance of collecting the right data is addressed in Chapter 5). New researchers often believe that they must do something new and original in their research, but drawing on or adapting or developing an existing piece of research is often very valuable and rewarding. Work that has focused on Key Stage 2, for example, could be adapted to look at the same issues in Key Stage 1. Undertaking similar work from a slightly different perspective or position is a useful way in which new findings and new ways of understanding learning and teaching can be discovered.

Chapter 3, then, is concerned with the ways in which you begin your work so that you can then structure your research in a systematic and purposeful way, keeping a clearly defined focus throughout.

Research is about deciding what question you want to ask and what information you will need in order to find the answers. Where you stand, how you look and what you look at will form the parameters of your research.

What is already out there?

When you undertake research into any aspect of education it is absolutely essential to be informed about what is already known about the area you are researching. A key element of any research project is the review of the literature – the existing research and scholarly perspectives which will inform your own research perspective and findings. Chapter 4 explains what the literature review is, its purpose in the research context and how to set about it in a systematic way. There is a great deal of research in education which is easily accessible through the Internet and this chapter will suggest ways in which you can make sure you find the most useful and significant pieces of research to review. You will need to be critical of what others have found out and ask questions about their approach and findings as part of the means by which you will understand and justify your own data. This chapter explains how to critique rather than criticise the work of others so that you can present a clear understanding of what research has already shown us about the element of practice you are researching.

The literature review identifies how and where your research is positioned in the context of what has already been examined and understood in your particular area of interest.

What approach should I take?

Once you have formulated a question and undertaken a review of what is already out there, you will need to think about the information that you will need to gather in order to answer your question. As explained earlier, Chapter 3 focuses on how to ask the right sorts of questions in small-scale school and classroom research so that the information you need to gather is easily accessible. If you ask questions which involve finding out about broad abstract concepts such as 'creativity', 'enjoyment' or 'engagement', it is much harder to identify and 'collect' data than if you frame your question so that you are looking to identify the specific, measureable impact on, say, spelling when approaching the teaching of writing in a particular way. Chapter 5 continues to develop this way of thinking by helping to clarify how you can be sure that the data collected will answer the question you have asked – if you want to know children's perspectives on, for example, mathematics investigations you will not need to collect any data from the teachers; if you want to know about the teachers' use of questioning in science you won't need to collect data from other subjects.

As you plan your data collection you will need to consider the research approach (or paradigm) which most suits the research you want to undertake. This is what you write about in the methodology section of your research report and this is the main focus for Chapter 5. The unique context of a primary school or classroom provides the perfect environment for research where insider knowledge (your knowledge of the school and the children, for example) can be brought to bear, as you are likely to be part of the social context being researched. This might also be described as a case study – you are looking at one small context (one school, one class, one child) and investigating it rather than undertaking large-scale research which might be more generalisable. There is also great potential in primary school classrooms for 'action research' – this is research which puts something new in place (having identified a need) and then evaluates the successfulness of the new approach as part of an on-going cycle. This chapter will help you understand how to structure your methodology chapter and will also reflect on the challenges involved in doing research with young children and the role of research ethics in ensuring that all research is respectful towards those participating in it.

All approaches have strengths and weaknesses, and in the methodology section of your research report you will need to justify the approach you have taken to collecting the data and why you collected the data that you did. You will also need to explain and justify the methods you used to collect the data (interviews, observations or other more unusual approaches) – Chapter 6 provides an overview of the research methods most frequently used in small-scale educational research.

Getting the right data is at the heart of a successful research project – you cannot find out what you want to know unless you have collected data which answers your question.

How will I collect the data?

There are countless books about research methods in education which explain the practicalities of the data collection process. There is no right way to collect data – if you are trying to discover something of the social world and the processes whereby individuals interact with one another you cannot simply and unproblematically say 'Well, I'll just ask them'. Other things come into play which inevitably impact on the answers you will be given. At a very basic level, if you, in a teacher role, ask children questions about their experiences in school they might well be nervous about offering what might be viewed as critical responses because you are in a powerful position relative to them. There are ways of mitigating against these sorts of issues, and some methods of collecting data put the children under less pressure to respond – for example, children can be asked to draw pictures or you can simply observe them as they engage in normal classroom activity. Chapter 6 outlines when and how interviews and questionnaires might be used most effectively to collect data but also explores other means by which data can be gathered. It also offers a model for critiquing different approaches and justifying the methods you have chosen in your research.

How you will collect the data you need requires careful consideration of the strengths and weaknesses of a range of research methods so that you can select and justify your approach.

How can I make sense of the data?

Once you have collected your data you will need to do more than simply report what you have found. The data analysis section of your research project is where you look closely at your data and ask yourself what it is telling you in relation to the question you asked. You might look for patterns, for similarities and differences between the responses; you might look to see whether boys and girls have responded noticeably differently; you might look closely at the language being used or the frequency of particular kinds of responses. Chapter 7 focuses on the data analysis you will be doing. In the analysis you might be looking for particular things that have been identified by others in the research you looked at as part of the literature review. You could draw on the same analytical frameworks (ways of looking at the data) that others have used and consider whether or how your findings mirror the findings of others. You might, however, look at what your data is telling you and come up with your interpretations which suggest other ways of looking, other ideas.

Whichever way you approach the analysis of your data you need to remain focused on your research question and ask what insights your data can give you. You will need to avoid being sidetracked by interesting, but irrelevant findings and you will need to examine your data thoroughly to see what it has to say. While you might well not be truly scientific in the way in which you do this, you will certainly need to be systematic and thoughtful in your approach. Chapter 7 will focus on how you can do this within the context of the small projects you have undertaken.

Working out what your data has to say will be the way in which you formulate arguments and ideas about what you are researching. The answers can be both affirming and challenging for your beliefs and practices in primary schools.

How do I write it?

When you write up your research as part of a course or to share your findings with the wider community, you are required to use an academic style and present your work in a certain structured way. The conventions you will be required to follow ensure that meanings are shared and understood (and you are demonstrating your academic ability and meeting the criteria for the qualification for which you are studying). For example, you will be required to reference what you have read so that you can demonstrate how and where your writing fits within the body of work which is already out there (you are acknowledging what is already in the stew before you add to it!).

You will be asked to follow a particular way of referencing so that anyone reading your work can see where your ideas have come from and can follow up the ideas or points you have made which draw on the work of others. If you don't reference correctly, it might look as if you are claiming other people's ideas as your own and the accuracy of your work can't be verified. Conventions like this and other aspects of academic writing are set out in Chapter 8.

Academic writing is a discipline which follows certain rules which must be followed so that you can demonstrate your understanding and make your contribution to the world of educational research.

Finally

Chapter 9 draws together the threads of the previous chapters in order to reiterate how the research you have done can be seen as hugely valuable as a prompt to adopt a 'researcherly disposition' as a teacher. It asks you to reflect on your learning through the research process. It also suggests ways in which you might disseminate your findings more widely within your school and beyond, and prompts you to think about ways in which you could build on your research in constructive ways.

Key features

In every chapter the authors draw on examples from research in practice which demonstrate aspects of the research process which they are discussing. This provides evidence of the practical application of the principles being expounded in this book. Each chapter begins by setting out its scope and purpose, and ends with some questions which will help guide you in the design, structure and writing of your research. Further reading is recommended throughout to help you develop elements of your research practice in greater depth.

References

Lave, J and Wenger, E (1991). *Situated Learning: Legitimate Peripheral Participation*. Cambridge: Cambridge University Press.

Lingard, B and Renshaw, P (2010). Teaching as a research-informed and research-informing profession. In Campbell, A and Groundwater-Smith, S (2010) (eds) *Connecting Inquiry and Professional Learning in Education: International Perspectives and Practical Solutions*. London: Routledge.

Further reading

Bell, J (2010) *Doing Your Research Project: A Guide for First-time Researchers in Education and Social Science*. Milton Keynes: Open University Press.

Burton, N, Brundrett, M and Jones, M (2008) *Doing Your Education Research Project*. London: SAGE.

Coles, A and McGrath, J (2010) *Your Education Research Project Handbook*. Harlow: Longman.

Hopkins, D (2002) *A Teacher's Guide to Classroom Research*. Milton Keynes: Open University Press.

Denscombe, M (2010) *Good Research Guide: For Small-scale Social Research Projects*. Maidenhead: McGraw Hill.

Greig, A, Taylor, J and MacKay, T (2012) *Doing Research with Children: A Practical Guide*. London: SAGE.

Hopkins, D (2002) *A Teacher's Guide to Classroom Research*. Milton Keynes: Open University Press.

Lambert, M (2012) *A Beginner's Guide to Doing Your Education Research Project*. London: SAGE.

Lankshear, C and Knobel, M (2004) *A Handbook for Teacher Research: From Design to Implementation*. Milton Keynes: Open University Press.

Opie, C (ed.) (2004) *Doing Educational Research: A Guide to First-time Researchers*. London: SAGE.

Roberts-Holmes, G (2014) *Doing Your Early Years Research Project*. London: SAGE.

Sharp, J (2009) *Success with your Education Research Project*. Exeter: Learning Matters.

Thomas, G (2009) *How to do your Research Project*. London: SAGE.

Chapter 2

What is evidence-based practice and why does it matter?

Judy Durrant

Objectives

This chapter:

- focuses on the practitioner researcher as a learner in their school and classroom context;
- examines the quest for evidence: 'what works' and the importance of 'why';
- emphasises realistic, interactive and effective research approaches that can be built into teaching, with direct impact on pupils' learning.

Chapter summary

A research-based approach to developing your practice provides you with evidence to effect change in your teaching, your classroom, your school, yourself and beyond.

Introduction

In my first few relentless, exhausting months of teaching, a friend from university who was in what I considered to be quite a high-powered job, said that she had been feeling a bit under the weather, so had decided to spend the day tidying her filing cabinet. I often recalled this when the inevitable viruses did the rounds, because I felt I did not have the luxury of planning 'down-time'. Every minute of the working day was filled; marking and planning loomed during evenings and weekends, on-going tasks built up if I did not keep on top of them, and I had to give my pupils nothing less than full attention, every lesson, every day. Demands on teachers have continued to increase, with greater internal as well as external scrutiny, and more focus on measurable outcomes and progress for which teachers are individually accountable. Adding more to teaching is therefore only reasonable if it is both valuable and realistic, if it helps you to meet the demands rather than adds to them and if it contributes to improvement.

This chapter makes the case for introducing a research orientation to your teaching, not as an optional extra, but as an essential and integrated dimension of effective professional practice. This involves consideration of different perspectives on evidence-based practice, taking the discussion to the heart of debates about what counts as reliable evidence, what constitutes 'good' research and why it matters. Embarking on your own enquiry not only prompts you to engage with wider educational research, but also enables you to use evidence from your own situation to enlighten your teaching and enhance children's learning. It should not be seen as something more to do, but as a different way of approaching your teaching, both individually and with colleagues. Many teachers have found that their experiences as researchers have changed their professional practice and perspective forever.

Teachers as learners

In any profession, there is an important responsibility to keep up to date with the latest ideas and information. Teachers have particular challenges in this respect: not only are there continuing changes in the nature of *what* is taught, but research and development inform pedagogy – *how* the teaching of this subject matter could be approached. Furthermore, new understandings continually arise from research into learning, leadership and school improvement, all of which influence what goes on in classrooms. A learning disposition is therefore crucial for teachers in order to take account of this changing knowledge and understanding, and develop new skills which may enhance practice. New phases of learning for teacher and student teacher alike, which can be prompted by embarking on a research and development project, are valuable not only for what is learnt about the theme in question, but also for the insights that come from being in the role of learner, perhaps grappling with a new methodology, resolving an ethical question, interpreting complicated evidence or working out a leadership strategy. Interesting conversations may arise if you reveal this to pupils who are part of your research; they may like to hear that by participating in your enquiry they are helping you with *your* learning.

New developments in educational knowledge and understanding are introduced against a backdrop of continually changing education policy. This does not always mirror contemporary changes in subject knowledge or research evidence in the discipline of education, while changes of emphasis in curriculum, professionalism and accountability come and go with different political regimes which are increasingly influenced by international developments and comparisons. There is therefore an additional necessity for teachers to maintain a working understanding of the policies that have implications for day-to-day practice and for planning, and it is also helpful to understand the bigger political picture which governs education reform and results in various initiatives that schools are required to implement. What happens in the classroom is subject to a wide range of influences. Understanding how an inspection framework has changed, or why reading is taught as it is, helps to make implementation of related policies more effective. However, teachers may also need to raise critical questions about educational purpose and process – what we do and why – in schools and classrooms.

Professional practice inevitably involves conflicts and dilemmas where your values and professional and political positioning seem to be at odds with what is required of you. Schools approach this in different ways, from an autocratic approach where full compliance is demanded and enforced, through to more inclusive styles of leadership where everyone is consulted before decisions are made. Inspection outcomes can sometimes demand a change of strategy. Approaches also depend on the nature of the change and its timescale. As a student teacher you might find yourself placed in settings where you meet these different approaches and can see how they influence how teachers approach their work with children. As a teacher, you may see contrasts as you take up a new post or when a new head teacher arrives.

A learning disposition can therefore be adopted at different levels. Learning everything that is asked of you, in order to implement policy within given frameworks, helps to ensure that your practice is effective and meets requirements. However, a genuine researcher's disposition might require you to ask deeper questions about policy, process, purpose and evidence for change. You can use research evidence to develop knowledge, understanding and skills that are adaptable for different situations and regimes, and can be expertly applied to unique school and classroom contexts. This helps you to contribute to the 'change conversation' in your school. By working collaboratively this can become a powerful process underpinning school development.

Example from practice

Alison, a teacher nearing the end of her Master's degree, said that it was the best thing she had ever done. Her classroom innovation, supported by enquiry, had resulted in an 'outstanding' grading in a recent observation, which had helped her to gain promotion. More important to her was that her enquiry approach, including reading, critical discussion and her own research, had helped her to understand the political forces at work and why she was under pressure individually and as a subject leader, as a result of the school being required to maintain high standards and levels of progress. She was now less inclined to take criticism or conflict personally and instead adopted a more analytical stance, working out why things happened the way they did and how she could take a more active role in school development. She described how she was able to help colleagues in her team to consider the implications of change and therefore plan more effectively. Having articulated her values and commitment clearly as a foundation for her research, she cut through the complexities of policy with fierce advocacy for her pupils.

Evidence-based practice can encompass many different kinds of professional learning, with a continuum from mechanistic and prescriptive training (for example, being trained how to implement a phonics scheme) through to approaches that can liberate you professionally, supporting individual agency, self-efficacy, voice and professional positioning, as Alison found out. Throughout your professional career you will come across all sorts of initiatives, models, programmes and packages which claim to have 'the answer' to a vexing issue. While there is a place for all kinds of answers, it is helpful to cultivate an awareness of the differences in what counts as evidence-based practice and ask critical questions as part of your professional learning, so that you can use that learning appropriately to understand the political and organisational context and motivation for changes you are asked to implement.

The quest for evidence

Educational research is subject to swings of fashion. At the turn of the twenty-first century, the British government funded small-scale teacher-led research projects through the 'Best Practice Research Scholarships' scheme (Furlong and Salisbury, 2005). A couple of years later, hundreds of schools and tens of thousands of teachers were involved in the National College for School Leadership's 'Networked Learning Communities' initiative, engaging in collaborative enquiry-based development within and between schools (Katz and Earl, 2010). At the time of writing, however, policy makers particularly value the evidence from large-scale studies involving statistically significant numbers of schools and pupils in experiments intended to determine 'what works' in education. These include 'randomised control trials' (RCTs) which apply a scientific approach to collecting data and aim to draw conclusions which can be replicated across contexts. One example of this is the 'Closing the Gap' project (see CUREE, 2015). The website describes the project as:

> the first ever attempt to use randomised trials to test multiple interventions simultaneously and at scale to close gaps. This will mean that the project will help reveal what works reliably in many contexts whilst helping us to work together to close gaps for vulnerable learners.

The aim of such projects is to be able to identify effective strategies that can be applied to inform improvement, but, as Welch (2015) points out, generalised conclusions from such studies need to be applied with an understanding of the effects of local conditions and cultural sensitivity to individual pupils and groups. It is individual teachers who are best placed to investigate how and why something may or may not work in a unique local setting – what a RCT broadly suggests will work might be qualified by your particular school or classroom or your pedagogical approach.

The Education Endowment Foundation (EEF), which provides funding for research and development to improve educational achievement, focusing particularly on children facing disadvantage, offers a 'Teaching and Learning Toolkit' where each theme or approach is graded according to cost, evidence and impact. In adopting one of these approaches, teachers might not have time to read the small print, but this is crucial in understanding what is being offered. The following is their note of caution on impact.

> *Crucially, the summaries in the Toolkit combine evidence from a range of different research studies into a single average for each area.* **This average will not necessarily be the impact of this approach in your school.** *Some of the approaches which are less effective on average might be effective in a new setting or if developed in a new way. Similarly, an approach which tends to be more effective on average may not work so well in a new context. However, we think that evidence of average impact elsewhere will be useful to schools in making a good 'bet' on what might be valuable, or may strike a note of caution when trying out something which has not worked so well in the past.*

> (EEF, 2015, 'Using the Toolkit')

This suggests that where such wider evidence is taken into account, distilling this into a recipe for success in all circumstances is not viable; all that might be available here is a 'good bet' to 'try out' in the light of experience. It may transform children's learning, but it may have no effect at all; it could even be counterproductive. In the EEF Toolkit, 'mastery learning' is shown as a low-cost, relatively effective strategy, which might be attractive to schools looking for quick gains on a tight budget, but again there is some important qualifying information to consider.

> *There are a number of meta-analyses which indicate that, on average, mastery learning approaches are effective, leading to an additional five months' progress over the course of a school year compared to traditional approaches. Unusually however, among the evidence reviewed in the Toolkit, the effects of mastery learning tend to cluster at two points with studies showing either little or no impact or an impact of up to six months' gain. This clear split and wide variation implies that making mastery learning work effectively is challenging.*

> (EEF, 2015, Mastery learning, 'How effective is it?')

Additional guidance follows: on collaborative learning, setting high expectations and children taking responsibility for their own learning. Finally, teachers are advised that the effectiveness of the approach decreases over time, so it should be used sparingly, perhaps for more challenging topics rather than for all lessons. Bypassing this advice and adopting the approach wholesale might therefore be disappointing and unhelpful.

While large-scale research findings may inform large-scale reform, application at local level is in the hands of schools and teachers, and the above example shows how important it is to adopt a critical perspective and delve beneath the headlines of the latest ideas and approaches so that evidence is not misunderstood. It is vital for teachers to be involved in examining the claims being made by studies underpinning improvement strategies: what is the evidence and how has it been analysed and qualified? However, there is more at stake than 'what works'; there is also the important question of why.

Purpose and accountability

The contradictions in the quest for 'what works' are explored by Biesta (2007) who argues that by focusing on the technical dimensions of educational process as problems to be solved, we omit the very essence of education as a democratic learning process. By limiting it, we undermine it. If we want children to be able to adopt critical perspectives, ask questions, be creative and make a contribution in school and in society, why would we train teachers to comply and conform to external requirements without the opportunity for critical discussion and consultation? Schools, professional bodies, individual teachers and student teachers need to ask not only 'what works?' but also 'what for?'. Large-scale reform and sometimes local initiatives are introduced on the basis of assumptions about the purposes of education. If the purpose of education is only for children to achieve well in tests and examinations, reforms and initiatives will be solely focused on this outcome. Research that serves this agenda will ask 'How can we get more children to pass tests at a higher level?'. Systematic, scaled-up research based on such assumptions can result in pared-down, reductionist findings – issues are distilled to their constituent parts and responses are geared towards the specified improvement, while ideas and approaches which fall outside the 'norm' or challenge the agenda are discounted. In contrast, teachers' own investigations tend to be focused on the real, individual concerns and needs of both adults and children, and can reveal diverse views about people's ambitions and values in the educational process. This often leads to a more holistic view of education in terms of learning, development and well-being. Often when teacher researchers set out to solve a practical problem through school-based investigation, these deeper questions and motivations surface, particularly through qualitative enquiry which engages with the perspectives of teachers and children. This can overturn assumptions about learning, teaching and schooling, presenting both challenges and contributions to the official agenda.

Opportunities for school-based research are therefore to be welcomed by student teachers, teachers and other practitioners because they create openings to ask the questions that underpin school structures, cultures and processes of change. Rather than being discomforting, you are likely find such investigations empowering as you discover the real stories and issues beneath the surface of teaching and learning activity. Children reveal perspectives you may never have considered before, and their comments can provide powerful and surprising insights; after all, they spend a great deal of time in your classroom. As a teacher or student teacher, you may discover very practical information, such as how uncomfortable it is to learn while sitting on the floor, or that children are getting hungry or too hot. Children may tell you what it is like to try to learn lessons that are not in their first language, or how important it is that friends on their table understand their dyslexia. Detailed, often qualitative, evidence from your own school challenges priorities and ways of working, and may suggest ways forward that better meet children's needs. The research approaches in this book will help you to ask the right questions. Research can be used to ask 'why?' as well as 'what?' involving colleagues, pupils and others in the conversation. As a student teacher you can adopt that 'researcher's disposition' we have already described so that you begin your career as a reflexive, questioning practitioner, but is never too late to start. Connecting with a project or programme that supports enquiry-based professional learning will give a framework within which to work.

Having made a case for asking deeper questions of purpose as well as process, there is a danger that becoming involved in research might sound rather subversive and revolutionary. Sometimes it is! However, the energy and enthusiasm that is generated through enquiry can always be put to positive and constructive use. As a teacher, it makes sense to link your research carefully with school priorities and understand and advocate its role within the school development process. This is likely to have much greater impact than using it to undermine leadership: use your research to *contribute* to leadership. The next chapter takes you through the process of developing your research idea. As a student teacher you might have more freedom to choose your research focus for more personal reasons, but whether you are a teacher or student teacher, you need to have clear purposes in mind, which may be focused on your own classroom and personal professional learning, or may have much greater scope. Sometimes there are also wider influences – for example, on other schools, within the community or network, or on education policy. As a student teacher you will be guided by tutors and by course demands as to the focus of your research, but you could also consider how you might work within your placement school's own development priorities. As an established teacher, by negotiating the focus of your investigation, perhaps with a senior leader or team leader, you can win support for your enquiry and leadership. This may be very practical support such as allowing time on the staff meeting agenda to talk to colleagues or enabling you to do some classroom observations, but it is also important to have encouragement, moral support and someone with whom you can talk through ideas either in your own school or elsewhere. Furthermore, it is reasonable to be held accountable for research undertaken in your own role and which might be funded or otherwise supported by your school. By working with people and thinking strategically, you will increase the power of the process and its eventual impact.

Researching to underpin change

In the context of the debate about what works and why, there is a wide range of benefits to researching your own practice, whether directly feeding into improvement through action research or, more broadly, gaining understanding and knowledge on themes of interest and relevance. This is why research is embedded into initial teacher education. As research becomes embedded in your practice you can gain a range of benefits.

Research can:

- help you find solutions to particular problems arising in your classroom or school;

- underpin professional learning of knowledge, skills and understanding;

- connect you with sources of information and networks of professional support;

- clarify purposes, processes and priorities when introducing change – for example, to curriculum, pedagogy or assessment;

- improve understanding of your professional and policy context, organisationally, locally and nationally, enabling you to teach and lead more strategically and effectively;

- develop your agency, influence, self-efficacy and voice within your own school and more widely within the profession.

Each of these can involve investigation using evidence from your own setting, along with wider research evidence. All fall under the helpful definition of research offered by Stenhouse (1975) of *systematic enquiry made public* which extends and enhances professionalism and practice. Where policy makers' emphasis may currently lie with large-scale studies such as randomised control trials, it is important to recognise the unique contribution that small-scale, teacher-led enquiry can make to educational research, and in turn to the educational process. Skilbeck has given a helpful explanation of Stenhouse's concept of teacher research as being concerned with gaining greater understanding of *the meanings, values, interests and concerns of people as expressed by them in real life situations* (1983, p11). This suggests detailed investigations that would be difficult to undertake as an outsider (someone who is not part of the context being researched) but would be enhanced by an insider's situational knowledge and use of existing relationships to further deep and meaningful enquiry about things that really matter to the school community. As a researcher in your own school, you also have the best understanding of how to make use of what you have learnt, whether personally or in supporting wider organisational development. In the context of new knowledge from wider research, it is only those directly involved in the educational process who can make it count in practice. It is these people – pupils, teachers, support staff, parents and others – whose feelings and attitudes matter when implementing change. Around this, there are unique local factors that make the introduction of recommended practices and policies different in every school. Improvement is therefore likely to be most effective if approached with a research orientation, an enquiry mind-set, asking questions, gathering evidence and involving people in collaborative enquiry as part of any process of change.

Evidence and impact

Too often, teacher and student-teacher research projects, perhaps particularly where part of an award-bearing programme such as a Master's degree or a PGCE, are reduced to an individual academic exercise. They can become bogged down in impenetrable methodological jargon, inappropriate discussions about validity, or ineffective and unimaginative approaches to data gathering and analysis, such that they sacrifice the clarity of purpose discussed at the start of this chapter. If the end result is only intended to be a paper submitted for assessment or published article, this may never engage anyone who can make practical use of the information. As a teacher you are well placed to design activities to engage and inspire colleagues with what you have learnt, without necessarily resorting to sitting them in rows listening to a slide-show presentation or giving them your essay to read. As a student teacher you can share ideas and evidence with your peers and take what you have learned with you into your teaching career. Mentors and placement colleagues will also be interested in your investigations. Remember that you will need to be sensitive and constructive in engaging people with new evidence and discussing the implications.

Choosing interactive research methods that are built into classroom practice and become part of the learning process can start to bring benefits to learners through the research process itself. With creative planning, the research can even become part of the curriculum. It may be helpful to focus not on findings leading to 'professional development' that may eventually lead to improvements in practice, but on improving practice directly. Participative enquiry approaches draw children increasingly to the centre of the research – their views and voices can lead the research in particular directions. This kind of approach can see the pupils as co-researchers – solving problems together as a class or school community. As a result, teachers and teaching assistants are more able to understand – and therefore plan – learning and teaching from the children's point of view. Research only has this powerful impact if it is planned that way. Dialogue about learning increases, children feel valued as teachers listen to their ideas, opinions and feelings, and relationships with learners improve. It is important to recognise the difference between this kind of approach and a more linear view of practitioner research which has the aim of finding out what works in relation to a particular problem and then implementing it – somewhat in isolation from the views of the children who will ultimately be affected. Interactive, participative projects designed to gather, use and share evidence during day-to-day activities are philosophically different: they involve a learning conversation and a leadership mind-set. By setting out with the intention of leading change underpinned by evidence, mapping intended outcomes and subjecting the process to continual critical review, these endeavours have greater potential to change the learning culture of your classroom and contribute to school development far beyond your original area of focus.

The following example illustrates how a deceptively simple question about the relative proportions of teacher talk and child talk resulted in some important developments led by three teachers from a primary school.

Example from practice

'Do we talk too much?': a teacher-led investigation into the relative value of teacher talk and child talk in class, within a whole-school action research project

Blean Primary School, Kent, worked with Canterbury Christ Church University to involve all teachers in year-long action research projects as part of the school improvement plan. Head teacher Lynn Lawrence recognised that it was important to *provide the framework for teachers to identify and implement improvements to teaching and learning for themselves* (CCCU, 2013, p2), building greater capacity for improvement based on enquiry, reflection and collaboration. Jane Martin, Karen Rockall and Matthew Buddle started with the research question 'How much can I talk in class?'. Their initial plan was to measure how much time children and adults spent talking but, having opened up the enquiry, they found the project was increasingly led by the children's needs. It was clear that children needed support in talking to one another and in using talk for learning, so different strategies were tried and evaluated by their own observations and judgements of what had changed.

In Jane's reception class, the children learnt active listening techniques, including the importance of eye contact. They responded to pictures, including their own drawings and other stimuli, in paired talk. They learnt a series of hand signals to give cues such as 'slow down', 'tell me more' or 'I don't understand' without interrupting the flow. Jane found that the youngest children could sustain discussion and develop one another's confidence in presentation using an innovative and popular approach that did not rely on adult intervention. The children were soon using these 'tools for talk' with enthusiasm to talk about their own pictures and work, and eventually taught them to Year 1 and Year 2 classes.

Karen used the National Geographic 'picture of the day' to develop language and generate questions, particularly focusing on the use of adjectives. The children's curiosity developed markedly around the scenes and topics introduced.

Matthew set up a 'conversation station', like a bus stop with pictures and questions which stimulated children to talk, value talk and listen to each other's ideas. When this was then moved into the corridor, it encouraged talk between children from different classes and age groups.

The teachers in this project group reported to colleagues that the project had led to a much greater proportion of talk, not only *by* children, but *led by* children.

It is important to note that individual teachers at Blean Primary School were given complete freedom to choose their focus for enquiry. They planned enquiry and gathered evidence on a wide range of themes which led to some important implications for school development, for example:

- highlighting issues for summer-born children, particularly the need to focus on leadership;
- encouraging growth mind-sets by celebrating what is learnt from mistakes;
- suggesting ways to use 'carpet time' more effectively;
- using active learning in mathematics in all year groups, not just with younger children;
- introducing mini 'brain breaks' to improve well-being;
- helping children to understand dyslexia through purchasing books to read together;
- involving children as partners in learning, developing a pupils' learning charter and undertaking learning walks;
- involving children in defining ethos and culture which unexpectedly revealed the importance of stillness and spirituality.

Across the school, the balance shifted noticeably towards greater involvement of children in their learning, as a result of their participation in teacher-led enquiry. Sometimes, it became child-led enquiry as assumptions were challenged and children were motivated by involvement in the enquiry itself. This was only possible because teachers were flexible, responsive and open to their evidence as it emerged, ensuring that improving learning was more important than carrying out research as originally planned. See CCCU (2013) for details of teachers' enquiries and Durrant (2014) for more about this approach to teacher-led development.

Evidence-based practice for school development

The example from Blean Primary School shows the crucial role of leadership in structuring and supporting school-based research. Many years of experience have demonstrated that schools can make most powerful use of internal enquiry combined with external research evidence where head teachers build action research and distributed leadership into the school improvement plan and link them explicitly with other initiatives and policy drivers. It helps if teachers are given freedom to choose their own areas of focus, sufficient funding is allocated for external support and time is provided for collaboration (however limited). Head teachers need to look for visible ways to value the work in progress and on completion, and can model enquiry by participating in the projects themselves, learning alongside their staff.

Teacher-led enquiry which engages with wider research as well as instigating school-based research can therefore generate much momentum for positive organisational change if the conditions are right. The following example illustrates how this can be tightly focused on one school improvement priority linked to professional standards and accountability, while still offering flexibility, choice and scope for unexpected outcomes. It describes a project that was designed to enable individual teachers' and teaching assistants' motivations and concerns to be aligned with school and national agendas and wider research evidence.

Example from practice

Effective assessment and feedback: using a whole school research project to address a school improvement priority

The head teacher of St Ursula's Catholic Junior School in the Diocese of Brentwood, Clare D'Netto, worked in partnership with Canterbury Christ Church University to involve all teachers and teaching assistants in action research to improve assessment and feedback. This responded to messages from wider educational research that effective feedback is one of the most important factors in improving learning and closing the attainment gap for the most disadvantaged pupils, and the project was linked to a priority in the school's action plan.

(Continued)

(Continued)

Under this broad area of focus, teachers and teaching assistants considered together what effective current practice looked like and how it would be evidenced, then generated a mass of questions from which collaborative action research projects emerged. This was an acknowledged risk for the head. As well as allowing considerable freedom in an area of accountability and professional standards, initial discussions led to the uncovering of inconsistencies and anomalies in marking and feedback. It was challenging to move from there to the initiation of enquiry and development projects, which relied on people's individual and collective commitment and energy.

Amid considerable 'messiness' (lots of flip-chart posters, sticky notes, challenging discussions and feeling a way forward), wider research on assessment was considered, assessment practices were reviewed and new strategies were trialled and evaluated. A great deal more dialogue with pupils was instigated, beginning to effect noticeable changes in classroom culture. Increased awareness of the children's individualised responses to oral and written feedback has led to much more personalised and sensitive approaches, recognising the psychological effects on children, both positive and negative. Early on, it was recognised that children wanted their work to be valued and that what the feedback looked like really mattered. They didn't like a lot of untidy red pen over their books; they thought the stamps used to show verbal feedback were a criticism; they didn't have time to act on the feedback received. Rather than prescription, policy has now been rewritten to allow for judgement and discretion in marking and feedback for different individuals. Teachers have noted their own shift from content-centred to child-centred teaching and have allowed more time to understand and act upon the feedback given. Children's fixed mind-sets have been challenged and *their perception of themselves as effective learners has grown* (CCCU, 2014, p7). Even in the year of the project the effects were seen in the improved levels of progress made, particularly for children identified as vulnerable and at risk of underachievement.

The head teacher has also noticed a professionalisation across the school during the course of the year. She noted, *My learning walks showed more and more good and outstanding practice by teaching assistants and teachers as they shared learning destinations with children. Colleagues were using assessment in classrooms as the bridge between teaching and learning* (ibid., p27). The action research enabled each teacher and teaching assistant to choose from a repertoire of assessment approaches suitable for different children and situations. Teaching assistants were motivated to create their own forum for discussion of the impact of their practice on pupils' attainment and progression. Teachers and teaching assistants wrote up their projects to gain recognition from the Teaching and Learning Academy. All the projects were shared at a conference attended by guests including local head teachers, while later the head teacher and teaching assistants presented their powerful story at a university conference.

Sharing the learning

In considering the purpose of researching your practice, it is important to think about wider uses and implications for your research from the outset, so that these can be planned for. The sharing of learning from teacher-led enquiry, in one school or a group of schools involved in a project, can be driven by a genuine desire to find out what others have been doing. Even if you are a confident teacher, it can be very daunting to lead a session for colleagues, but often learning from evidence and activity in your own school is the best way to move practice forwards and you should be able to count on their respect and support. As a student teacher, you may share your learning as part of your course. Make the most of help and guidance from within a school-based project from your tutor or mentor. A useful basic principle is to use your whole repertoire of professional skills to inspire colleagues' learning. A slide-show presentation might be considered as a last resort or capture key points for future reference. Development activities designed by teacher researchers in the examples above have involved the following.

- Drawing each other's portraits in pairs and giving each other feedback.

- Modelling with spaghetti and marshmallows.

- Making collages.

- Slideshow of children's photographs, 'What makes our school special?' with popcorn.

- A game show presenting research evidence: 'Who wants to be a summer-born child?

- Videos of children giving feedback on teachers giving feedback.

- A 'field trip' around the school environment.

- Listening to an account of an observed day in the life of a child with dyslexia.

- Sitting on the carpet to see what it feels like.

- A quick-fire quiz with a buzzer and chocolate prizes.

- A competition to solve a geometrical puzzle in teams.

- Making body sculptures of mathematical shapes, accessorised with sports equipment.

Such activities generate a great deal of laughter, but also thinking and discussion. The activities have challenged practice in a non-threatening way, are very memorable and strengthen relationships. Colleagues have to support each other, for example, where anxieties surface, there is disagreement or people find themselves unable to complete a task. It is always fascinating, as a teacher, to reflect on being a learner. It is important to allow substantial time for reflection at the end of such development activities – for example, selecting three learning points and one action point. During the reflection times, the chatter invariably dissolves into silence and deep thought as teachers have valued one another's contributions and are taking away some important ideas and messages. It is encouraging when colleagues can learn from what you have done and found out.

If as a teacher researcher you do not have a ready-made opportunity to share what you have learnt, see if you can create one. You might talk to a mentor or senior leader responsible for professional development, or offer an informal invitation to visit your classroom for a discussion with tea and cake, or use a ready-made forum such as a team meeting, or write a brief summary for the school bulletin, or put a poster in the staffroom with children's quotations. Once you have developed confidence, and if you have funding, there are also opportunities to engage with the educational research community beyond your school. For example, the UK's National Teacher Research Panel publishes research summaries on its website (NTRP, 2015) and some annual conferences such as the British Educational Research Association (BERA) and the International Congress of School Effectiveness and Improvement (ICSEI) include a practitioner research day. We revisit this and other ideas in the final chapter.

Evidence-based practice: the way forward

Getting involved even individually in school-based enquiry to improve the evidence-base for your practice can lead to important changes to your teaching and your pupils' learning. Sometimes, with support and planning, you can make significant impact on your school. Collaborating with colleagues, from your own school or elsewhere, can make an even greater impact and enable you to share your learning more widely. Often there are unexpected wider outcomes, even if the original aim was to solve specific problems in learning and teaching. Where research-engaged approaches are built into school improvement plans and supported by strong leadership, teacher-led, enquiry-based developments can lead to profound cultural change.

Making changes without a foundation in evidence is not worth the risk. It is important to look at wider evidence from reports, journals, books and websites, to provide the theoretical context for your own enquiry. If this sounds daunting, there are useful digests available that will give you shortcuts to current information and ideas, and you can look out for the current round of courses and conferences which pick up key themes. Collaborate with colleagues to share the load; your school should have a strategy for this (and if not, you might suggest it). A stronger foundation in evidence, both from wider research and school-based enquiry, can help schools to meet the challenges of external accountability and interpret policy requirements for unique contexts, while improving relationships, environments and organisational cultures for both teachers and learners through carefully and creatively planned research and development processes. The evidence generated and interpreted by teacher researchers offers a unique contribution to this process in each school setting. What you 'find out' is important, but your purpose, how you approach your enquiry and what you do with your evidence is what really counts.

Things to think about

1. Which of the following aspects of research in practice would be *most* valuable to you:

   - problem-solving a particular classroom issue?

   - improving your professional knowledge, skills or understanding?

- clarifying your professional purposes and priorities in the context of school and national policy?

- increasing your personal confidence, autonomy and self-efficacy?

2. Is there a clear distinction between effective practice and evidence-based practice?

3. What 'hot topic' would you like to investigate in your current role? How would you start?

4. What support does your school give to teacher-led enquiry and development? How could you encourage this?

5. How could you collaborate with colleagues to keep up with the latest educational research?

References

Biesta, G (2007) Why "What works" won't work: Evidence-based practice and the democratic deficit in educational research. *Educational Theory*, 57: 1–22.

Canterbury Christ Church University (CCCU) (2013) Learning Together to Enjoy and Achieve: Action research to improve learning and teaching at Blean Primary School, 2012–13. Available from: www.canterbury.ac.uk/education/our-work/research-knowledge-exchange/themes/professional-organisational-and-leadership-development.aspx (accessed September 2015).

Canterbury Christ Church University (CCCU) (2014) Effective assessment and feedback: A risky journey. Available from: www.canterbury.ac.uk/education/our-work/research-knowledge-exchange/themes/professional-organisational-and-leadership-development.aspx (accessed September 2015).

CUREE (2015) Centre for the Use of Research and Evidence in Education. Available at: www.curee.co.uk (accessed September 2015).

Durrant, J (2014) 'Children see differently from us': A fresh perspective on school improvement. *Professional Development Today,* 16(2).

EEF (2015) Education Endowment Foundation website. Available from: https://beta.educationendowmentfoundation.org.uk (accessed November 2015).

Furlong, J and Salisbury, J (2005) Best practice research scholarships: An evaluation. *Research Papers in Education*, 20(1): 45–83.

Goodnough, K (2008) Dealing with messiness and uncertainty in practitioner research: The nature of participatory action research. *Canadian Journal of Education*, 31(2): 431–58.

Katz, S and Earl, L (2010) Networking and collaboration for school improvement. *School Effectiveness and School Improvement: An International Journal of Research, Policy and Practice.* 21(1): 27–51.

National Teacher Research Panel (2015) Available at: www.ntrp.org.uk (accessed September 2015).

Skilbeck, M (1983) Lawrence Stenhouse: Research methodology: Research is a systematic enquiry made public. *British Educational Research Journal*, 9(1): 11–20.

Stenhouse, L (1975) *An Introduction to Curriculum Research and Development*. London: Heinemann.

Welch (2015) A call to action: Let schools drive research. *Times Educational Supplement*, 2 October, 20–1.

Further reading

Hammersley, M (2007) *Educational Research and Evidence-based Practice*. London: SAGE.

Kincheloe, J L (2003) *Teachers as Researchers: Qualitative Inquiry as a Path to Empowerment*. London: RoutledgeFalmer.

Pollard, A (2008) *Reflective Practice: Evidence-informed Professional Practice*. London: Bloomsbury Academic.

Pring, R (2004) *Evidence-based Practice in Education*. Milton Keynes: Open University Press.

Taber, KS (2007) *Classroom-based Research and Evidence-based Practice: A Guide for Teachers*. London: SAGE.

Chapter 3

Making a contribution to knowledge: where do I begin?

Rebecca Austin

Objectives

This chapter:

- helps you decide on the focus for your research project;
- guides you towards formulating a question within your area of interest;
- provides you with a starting point for coherent, systematic empirical research.

Chapter summary

Research is about deciding what question you want to ask and what information you will need in order to find the answers. Where you stand, how you look and what you look at will form the parameters of your research.

Introduction

There is a great outdoor activity you can do with children. You give them a small, rectangular frame made out of four strips of cardboard and you ask them to use this to pick out a section of the outdoor environment on which they will focus. It is a way of getting children to look closely at just a small section of the outside without being distracted by everything else around them. This chapter aims to help you frame your research in much the same way, so that you are clear about what it is you are looking at. The process of doing this can be seen as deciding what lies outside your focus – what you are going to ignore – as much as deciding what is within the frame.

Research always involves loss – you can't do everything! From the very beginning of your project you need to resign yourself to what you cannot do within the timescale, the length and the context of your project. And even once you have collected your data you will have to make further decisions about what to lose because there will be fascinating things that you discover from your data that fall outside the scope of what you are able to write about for your particular purpose.

When using their cardboard frame, children are encouraged to find unusual or unexpected ways of looking at their environment, zooming in close or looking from the side or underneath. This is a good way to think about how you might approach your research: finding a way of looking that could show you things you might not usually notice or consider. We can think of it as *making the familiar strange* (Barnes and Shirley, 2007) and this chapter will help you consider ways in which you can take a similar approach with your research.

Where do I begin?

When you write up your research you will set it out in a particular way (the following chapters in this book take you through each of the sections which you will write) – the first section is the introduction. Your introduction will tell your reader why you chose to research this particular aspect of practice, give a brief summary of the current context for this area and provide an overview of how you went about your research. The introduction might touch on a personal element such as your own experiences in school as a child, your observations in school contexts or a personal passion or interest, but will then move towards putting this in an academic or scholarly frame.

Deciding what you want to research is likely to take a little time and thought. If you are writing a Master's dissertation or longish project (15,000 words or more) you might have the luxury of a little more time to think about what you want to research and you are also likely to have more time available to collect and analyse data. In addition, the longer the timescale and word limit for your project, the more data you can collect, knowing you will have the time and words to do it justice in the writing up. If, however, you are undertaking a short classroom-based investigation which might typically be written up in just 5,000 or so words, you will need to be canny in the design and framing of your research so that you can demonstrate a depth of understanding about a small aspect of primary practice rather than simply skimming the surface of something too broadly conceived. Using a question to frame your research is crucial – it sets the parameters for your research and ensures that it keeps to a clearly defined focus. However, getting it right takes some preparation and thought.

The research question

The first thing to consider is what it is that you want to know more about. As was explained in Chapter 2, it might be that you don't have a completely free hand. You might be working within a module or programme which has already narrowed the field to something like inclusion, primary PE or co-operative learning, or your school might have asked you to research a particular area related to the school development plan. Nevertheless, however your research has come about, it is likely there will be some room for manoeuvre so that you can give it a personal twist – the best small-scale research such as the one you are engaged in comes from a genuine desire to find out more about something or understand something better.

So you could start by thinking about something that has interested or puzzled you from your own experiences in the classroom, either in relation to your prescribed focus or, if you have a free hand, from your broader experience in schools. This might include something that you think could be done better or something you want to understand more fully – for example:

- Why do children get 10/10 in spelling tests but always spell the same words wrongly in their writing?

- Why do some children find learning to tell the time so difficult?

- How can I get children to ask more questions?

- What makes outdoor learning so appealing to some children?

- What do children actually learn in my role-play area?

- What role do teachers' personal beliefs play in teaching religious education?

- How does children's physical development affect their learning?

- How can I best support children with English as an additional language (EAL) in science?

- How can I improve children's independent problem-solving in maths?

- Do mixed ability groups work for all learners?

- Why is reading aloud to children seen to be so important?

Questions such as these are not your research question yet; they are simply a starting point for thinking about the activities which take place in your classroom and pinpointing an area of interest. They get the juices flowing and should be things you find yourself mulling over when you aren't even thinking about your research as such. They are genuine areas of interest about your practice.

Another way to find a starting point is to write down on individual sticky notes ten or more areas of general interest such as:

- boys' writing;

- mathematical investigations;

- teachers' questions;

- children's literature;

- dialogic talk;

- children's drawing;

- dyslexia;

- classroom displays;

- differentiation;

- progression in science;

- guided reading;

- using primary sources in history;

- drama.

These areas can be anything at all that interests or intrigues you – to do with subjects, learning in general, the learning environment, teaching strategies, assessment – or something completely esoteric based on a personal interest. Mineralogy, Minecraft™, Lego™, pottery, photography, cookery and stamp collecting might all be things which could form the basis for investigating primary practice. With the sticky notes in front of you, sort them into different groups or pairs and see if there are particular combinations which you are drawn to. You might come up with:

- children's drawings and progression in science;

- teachers' questions and map work;

- Minecraft™ and boys' writing;

- children's literature, differentiation and guided reading;

- Lego™ and mathematical investigations;

- patterns in mathematics and art and nature;

- ability grouping, dialogic talk and using primary sources in history learning;

- photography and learning outside the classroom.

Again, these are not your actual research questions, rather they begin to sharpen your focus. This approach also begins to set up the possible ways in which you might go about collecting data. As you look at the questions above you can see how they could be put into practice by:

- asking boys to write a story based on their experiences of using Minecraft™;

- looking at children's drawings of scientific concepts to see how they represent children's developing understanding;

- recording teachers' questions when teaching map work;

- using carefully chosen texts of different difficulty with children in guided reading;

- setting up mathematical investigations using Lego™;

- using patterns in art and nature to explore mathematical patterns;

- using primary sources in history to stimulate dialogic talk in groups;

- asking children to take photographs of things they like doing outdoors.

Of course, there are many other ways you could go about investigating these areas – you are simply developing your thinking a little further. You can probably think of at least one other way each of the above could be approached. At this point you really want to start feeling excited about your potential research project and have some ideas about what you might do to investigate your chosen area.

Researcher bias

When you set out to research something it might be the case that it is something that you already feel very strongly about. You might have a belief about certain practices or approaches which you think are particularly effective or particularly 'wrong'. You can, of course, research these areas but you need to think carefully about the bias that you might bring to the project. If you think that mixed ability grouping is more effective than grouping by ability before you start the research it might become a self-fulfilling prophecy – you might see what you are looking for in the data, or you might even set up the project in such a way that it can only show one particular outcome.

The purpose of researching something which you already 'believe', however, is that it gives you evidence to support your belief. Instead of simply saying that you think something is so, you can say 'my research suggests', which adds weight to what might otherwise simply be personal opinion. This is revisited in later chapters but needs to be highlighted here.

Dipping a toe into the literature

The next step is a vital one – you need to start to explore the field. Before you dive headlong into your research you need to get a flavour of what is already out there – how others have looked at the area you are interested in and what they have to say about it. When you write up your research, the first main section is the literature review which examines existing research and scholarly understandings which relate to your own research project. The next chapter of this book guides you through how to approach this. At the very beginning of your research, though, you are not doing a full literature review, you are simply taking a broad sweep through the literature to get a feel for what is already understood in the key areas you want to examine. In doing this you will find that you narrow your interest further as you read about other research projects and how they have been executed, and begin to think about areas which might bear closer examination, or you might begin to see where there are possible gaps in the field – things that appear not to have been researched very much or in detail. Of course, it is also possible that as you read around the area you realise that it is not quite what you thought, or that you are not as interested in that particular topic as you thought you were, which is good! It means that you can then go to your next question, your next sticky notes combination and start reading up around that, having eliminated a non-starter.

You might also discover that the area that interests you is already widely researched – that the existing field is immense. This is not a problem *per se*, but it might mean that there is a great deal of reading which needs to be done which might be outside the scope of the time you have available. In addition, you might find that the specific area which you wanted to investigate is already very well researched and understood – with a broad consensus among researchers. While you might be put off by this, you could also use it to your advantage. Where a great deal is already understood about a particular aspect of education, you can really hone the focus for your research. For example, boys' reading choices have been very widely researched – including large-scale, funded projects – but you could look at boys reading graphic novels, girls reading non-fiction (surprisingly under-researched!), Year 6 high achieving boys and their online reading practices, boys' interactions with books in nursery settings. All of these will link to existing research but you will add something extra from the specific context in which you are working.

You could also choose to re-create a research project which you have read about and found of particular interest, which can enable you to offer fresh insights from the data you gather in your context. This might involve a slight adjustment to the research methods or the approach to the analysis based on your reading of the research and how you think it might be developed. The concluding section of research reports in journals and elsewhere often suggests areas for further study (just as you will do in the conclusion to your own research) and you could use these suggestions to shape your study. This is often a good way to approach a small-scale classroom investigation. Existing research in the field will be indicated in the report's literature review – you will simply need to update it and you can offer a focused critique for your particular approach within your methodology section based on how the researchers approached their project. You will also have findings and conclusions from their research which will be directly comparable to your own.

Example from practice

Burnett and Myers, writing in 2002, state in their conclusion to their journal article which reports on their research about children's out-of-school literacy practices:

There is clearly a need for further similar research with different age groups in different settings to gain greater insights into the breadth of children's literacy preferences.

(Burnett and Myers, 2002, p62)

You could read their research, identify how the children and setting where you would be working could offer a different perspective, and then use the same approach and analytical frame as them (approaches to analysis are explained further in Chapter 7) to structure your research. You would also be able to identify how, in the years since their research, the world of out-of-school literacy practices have changed, drawing on other research which has since investigated this and thus contributes to an ongoing debate. You certainly shouldn't see taking this approach as any less valid or challenging than taking an original perspective – and being truly original in educational research is not easy!

In order to find out what has already been written, you might search your institution's library catalogue and/or an academic search engine such as Google Scholar™ (the next chapter also discusses how to go about using tools such as these) using the key words from your sticky notes or your broad research question in various combinations to identify the most recent, relevant and most highly cited research. You are really looking for journal articles from peer-reviewed journals which report on research which has been undertaken. The next chapter provides more details about how to go about finding the most appropriate work to look at. This initial sweep of the field gives you a starting point to see what is out there and can be a source of inspiration and further excitement.

Getting focused

The temptation when doing research is to take a belt-and-braces type approach – set a broad question to investigate, collect lots of data and then see what you can glean from all the information you have gathered. In reality, this can lead to an unfocused mess – you have so many things that you could write about that you end up skimming the surface and not really getting your teeth into anything of real substance. The more focused and precise you are about what you are looking at, the more potential there is to examine your data in detail to see what it is telling you. You are not trying to change the world; you are trying to find something out about something – something that you can add to all the other somethings that are known or understood or speculated about so that you make a contribution to knowledge. In the context of your research the size or reach of your contribution is not important. You are able to offer valuable insights about one small element of primary practice and that is enough!

From a pragmatic perspective, the other reason that you are probably undertaking this research is as part of the assessment for a particular qualification. While the big picture is that you are contributing to the research field (and your own personal knowledge and understanding and practice), there is also the consideration that you are showing that you know and understand how to go about research, and that you can meet the criteria by which you are being assessed. Chapter 8 revisits this and helps you ensure that you are writing up your research in such a way that you address the different purposes which your report will serve.

There are certain things to think about as you begin to really narrow down your question. You need to think about who can participate in your research (who are you able to ask?) and the sort of data that you will be able to access. If you want to research something about children for whom English is an additional language, for example, you need to be sure that you will be able to work with such children. In addition, Chapter 5 talks you through the ethical considerations you will need to take into account when doing research in primary schools and this might well affect your data. For example, if you are not given permission to record children talking, then you might prefer, if possible, to collect written or drawn data; sensitive issues are likely to be off-limits, and if you are critiquing an element of practice in your school you might need to consider how your question is phrased so that teachers who participate do not feel that you are judging them negatively.

The research question

Throughout this chapter I have referred to your 'research question' – as I have explained, this will be the focus for what you want to find out. You might read articles and research reports where the title is not phrased as a question. When you look more closely, though, you will see that the research was based on a particular question but has been reported as what has been found out.

> ### Example from practice
>
> The title of the Burnett and Mayers (2005) research described earlier is '"Beyond the Frame": exploring children's literacy practices'. Their stated research question, though, is: *What do children identify as significant in their uses of literacy?* (p57). This is developed further into two even more focused subquestions. Although the title has avoided the use of the direct question, the question is clearly evident in their report and, along with the subquestions, has provided the focus and structure for their approach.

Different kinds of questions set up different kinds of projects. Chapters 5 and 6 take you through the ways in which the question you have set leads to certain methodologies and methods (the kind of data you collect and the ways in which you collect it), and in turn this influences the way you analyse your data. We will address elements of this here as well. Research is a recursive process and you cannot consider your research question without having at least some idea of how you might go about it and how you will interpret your data. Your research question might be very clearly focused on a particular group of participants such as 'high achieving boys' and 'primary music teachers', and there are likely to be pragmatic limits on the number of participants. For small-scale projects you are unlikely to want more than the equivalent of one class of participants, and in most cases you are likely to be working with much smaller numbers.

If you set up research questions, which indicate that the group of children or teachers on whom you will focus, you also narrow the scope for analysis. If you ask 'What do high achieving boys read outside school?' you can *only* look at high achieving boys and any comparisons with girls out of school reading or low achieving boys out of school reading will need to be done by drawing on the findings of existing research, which might not be appropriate for your context. That's not to say you shouldn't do this. Again, in research, you need to demonstrate your awareness and understanding – so as long as you are clear about what the issues are and how you have accounted for them in your research, you can go ahead with almost any question. You could, however, rephrase it as: 'What do children read outside of school?' Doing this enables you to collect data from, say, the whole class of children, and you can then look at what your data is telling you and consider whether there are significant differences between different groups of children. You have left room for some flexibility in the interpretation of the data. If it turns out that there is something really significant about high achieving boys out of school reading, then you can highlight this in your analysis and discussion.

Other helpful ways to phrase questions include:

- What are children's/teachers' perceptions of . . . ?

- How do . . . ?

- In what ways . . . ?

These kinds of questions or titles tend to be focused on an existing element of practice which will be examined in more detail. The aim is to find out more about how things are in order to develop a rich understanding so that you can comment on effective practice or suggest developments for the future. This approach is a good one if you are fairly limited for time, or you think you might encounter some barriers or opposition to introducing something new in the classroom to research.

You can add another layer to this kind of research by making it a comparative study – looking at approaches in different Key Stages, for example. As before, though, you could simply collect data from both KS1 and KS2 and interpret the data from a range of perspectives, including the different Key Stages. As soon as you add a comparative element to any research you are adding to your workload in terms of collecting data and writing about it. You might want to think carefully about this. If you have to describe two different activities or approaches or contexts and then analyse two (or more) sets of data, you are giving yourself double the work. It is not necessary to offer a comparison but it might be that you feel that this is particularly pertinent to your research. For example, if you were looking at children's conceptual development in science, it is likely to be essential to have data from children of different ages.

You might, however, want to try out something new or different as part of your research. This might be something that has arisen from your initial thoughts and readings. Perhaps you want to try a different approach to teaching spelling; you might want to see what happens when you teach art outdoors; you might want to increase opportunities for mark-making in the role-play area or you might want to explore children's problem-solving in design technology. In this case, you will be setting up a question which might use phrases such as:

- What is the effect of . . . ?

- To what extent does . . . ?

- What are children's responses to . . . ?

A possible issue with this sort of question is that it might require some kind of comparative data – either from previous practice or by setting up a control or comparison group. As above, this can increase the timescale required, the amount of data you need and the number of words you need to do it justice. You don't always have to have the comparative data, however – once more this is something you need to justify in your writing. For a small-scale investigation, it is perfectly acceptable to simply try out an idea and reflect on children's responses to it – you do not always have to make comparisons.

It is worth remembering that your question will rarely, if ever, begin with 'why?'. 'Why?' is the question you ask during the analysis of your data. Why did drama have this effect? Why do photographs support children's outdoor learning? Your research question is more likely to ask 'what?' or 'how?' so that you can think about the 'why?' in your discussion of the data.

A good rule of thumb is to make sure that your question cannot be answered with a 'yes' or 'no' – this can make for a *very* short research report!

- Do boys choose to read more non-fiction than fiction?

- Is there a difference between girls' and boys' attitudes to competitive sport?

- Do teachers ask open-ended questions in science?

The methodology and analysis chapters in this book review the implications of the above discussions in more detail. At this point, though, you should just bear them in mind as you formulate your question – you will need to know the shortcomings of your question and the subsequent research as well as the strengths. There is no such thing as the perfect research project – you simply have to make sure you justify the approach you have taken.

Getting the question right

There isn't a magic formula for coming up with a good question and sometimes it can take quite a while to get it exactly how you want it. When you read research reports the title of the journal article, as mentioned earlier in relation to the Burnett and Myers article, might not be the actual research question and it is often a play on words related to the findings – so don't be fooled!

Example from practice

'Views from inside the shed: young children's perspectives of the outdoor environment' (Clark, 2008) is the title of a journal article. The research question, however, is not revealed until the beginning of the analysis section: 'What can young children reveal about their priorities and interests in outdoor spaces attached to early childhood provision?' (Clark, 2008, p352).

Your research question will usually also be your title in the context of a small-scale assignment, but for a journal article, dissertation or thesis you might play around with the words and ideas to create a more catchy title.

You are trying to formulate a question which is a straightforward and transparent explanation of what you want to find out. It needs to be precise and detailed so that you maintain a clear focus. Let's take the following as an example:

How does drama improve children's creative writing?

As we unpick this we will see why it is far too broad and unfocused as a research question, although on the surface it seems quite reasonable. The first point is, of course, that there is an underlying assumption that drama *does* improve children's creative writing. This is not always a problem – earlier in this chapter we considered researcher bias and positionality – and it might be that in the introduction to your research you will explain that there is a broad consensus from research that drama *does* improve creative writing, which is why you have phrased the question as you have. As with most things in education, there are few black-and-white answers, but you need to have answers for the sorts of questions that whoever is reading your research report might ask. If I saw a research question like this, I would certainly want some justification for the underpinning assumption.

So, leaving that to one side the next issue is the word 'drama'. There are a myriad ways in which drama is understood and used in primary classrooms. In a research project of the kind you are undertaking you are unlikely to have the opportunity to try out lots of different kinds of drama – for small-scale projects with a word count of 4,000–5,000 words you are likely to collect data from perhaps one or two lessons. So you need to be much more precise. Perhaps you are going to use hot-seating? Decision alley? Improvised off-page conversations? Even then, who is going to be hot-seated – teacher or children? What sorts of decisions are going to be the focus of the decision alley? What is the context for the drama? Put all this in the question with as much precision as you can.

How does hot-seating children as the villain in traditional tales improve their creative writing?

It's starting to take shape but there is still a way to go! The next word we're going to wrestle with is 'improve'. If you want to look at improvement, then you need some 'before' data as well as 'after' (as discussed earlier). This then becomes a form of comparative project and you need a way of measuring the difference between the two datasets. In addition, you will need to be confident that it is the *drama* that has contributed to the improvement and be able to identify that specifically for your reader. That is, you can't take a piece of writing done three months earlier as part of an assessment which required children to write without support and compare it with the writing they do following the drama lesson you do with them for your research. It simply isn't a fair comparison. It could, however, be quite tricky to try to find something the children have already done which is comparable. You could decide to teach two groups of children, one with the drama and one without. Is this a fair test, though? You could balance the groups in terms of ability, but you would need to make sure the non-drama group had a comparable input. You can't do exciting drama with one group and a dull, teacher-led input for the other and use that to say that the group which did drama produced better writing – of course they will! The simplest thing is to remove the word 'improve' altogether and ask something about impact, influence, effect or similar, so:

What is the effect of hot-seating children as the villain in traditional tales on their creative writing?

This is beginning to look good! Notice how we have changed the beginning of the question in order to accommodate this different emphasis and we now have a question which is very focused in terms of hot-seating/villains but will support an exploration of the 'effect' which could be quite broad-ranging. There is scope here perhaps to see things we weren't expecting, and it is a genuine question.

We now come to the last bit: 'creative writing'. Whenever I see the word 'creative' in a research question I have some concerns – creativity is such a contested, difficult to pin-down term. What do we mean by 'creative writing'? In English lessons it is often used to mean story writing – and arguably some stories are very lacking in creativity in its broader sense. How can 'creativity' be identified, measured, judged? What you are really interested in here, perhaps, is how they write in response to the teaching strategy you have used and what elements of that writing might specifically be attributed to the drama activity. Hot-seating requires children to go into role, empathise with the character and 'be' them, putting their thoughts, motivations and ideas into words. So, if hot-seating is successful, children might show this by being able to write a piece which clearly demonstrates the voice which represents the character (Grainger et al., 2005).

Let's add this to our question:

What is the effect of hot-seating children as the villain in traditional tales on their written representation of the character's voice?

The use of 'what is the effect of?' in this way also allows you to look for other things such as we discussed earlier – you might consider boys' and girls' responses to see if this seems significant; the difference between high- and low-attaining writers' work; any differences between the different villainous characters which were used.

What we have now is a question which very clearly identifies what the research project is about and pretty much sets up the approach that you will take.

- You will hot-seat children as the villain in one or more carefully selected traditional tales.

- You will ask them to do some writing in the first person as the villain.

- You will look at the way in which they have used a 'voice' for the character.

- You will discuss how the drama has affected this (for example, you might find that particular words and phrases from the hot-seating are reproduced in the writing; that vocabulary used is precise and effective in demonstrating empathy).

Your reader, right from the outset has a really good idea of what your project is about and what to expect from your research report.

Things to think about

1. The timescale and word count for your project will be a significant influence on the breadth and depth of the research you can undertake. What is realistic for you within the context of your investigation?

2. What are the puzzles, niggles, frustrations, excitements or passions that you have experienced so far in your time in school? What elements of practice and interest can you combine? Can you begin to formulate tentative questions about these areas? How might you go about investigating them?

3. To find a focus for your research you need to combine a personal interest with existing research in the field so that you can contribute to what is already known about that particular element of primary practice. How does existing research help narrow your focus further?

4. What are your biases and preconceptions? What will you need to be aware of as you undertake the research?

5. Does your question clearly identify the elements of your research and indicate to the reader the main aim and focus for your investigation? Have you removed any ambiguous or misleading terms?

6. Does your question provide a narrow focus for the collection of data but broad potential scope for analysis?

References

Barnes, J and Shirley, I (2007) Strangely familiar: Cross-curricular and creative thinking in teacher education. *Improving Schools*, 10(2): 162–79.

Burnett, C and Myers, J (2002) 'Beyond the frame': Exploring children's literacy practices. *Reading*, 36: 56–62.

Clark, A (2007) Views from inside the shed: Young children's perspectives of the outdoor environment. *Education, 3–13*, 35(4): 349–63.

Grainger, T, Goouch, K and Lambirth, A (2005) *Creativity and Writing Developing Voice and Verve in the Classroom*. London: RoutledgeFalmer.

Further reading

Bell, J (2010) *Doing Your Research Project: A Guide for First-time Researchers in Education and Social Science*. Milton Keynes: Open University Press.

Brown, S, McDowell, L and Race, P (1995) *500 Tips for Research Students*. London: Kogan Page.

Coles, A and McGrath, J (2010) *Your Education Research Project Handbook*. Harlow: Longman.

Cryer, P (2006) *The Research Student's Guide to Success*. Milton Keynes: Open University Press.

Hopkins, D (2002) *A Teacher's Guide to Classroom Research*. Milton Keynes: Open University Press.

Lambert, M (2012) *A Beginner's Guide to Doing Your Education Research Project*. London: SAGE.

Lankshear, C and Knobel, M (2004) *A Handbook for Teacher Research, From Design to Implementation*. Milton Keynes: Open University Press.

Opie, C (ed.) (2004) *Doing Educational Research*. London: SAGE.

Roberts-Holmes, G (2014) *Doing Your Early Years Research Project*. London: SAGE.

Sharp, J (2009) *Success with Your Education Research Project*. Exeter: Learning Matters.

Chapter 4

The literature review: what is already out there?

Viv Wilson

Objectives

This chapter:

- explains what a literature review is, its purpose in the research context and how to set about it in a systematic way;
- introduces the distinction between reading critically and criticising;
- considers how to plan your literature review to discuss the key themes from your reading in order to support your own research study.

Chapter summary

The literature review identifies how and where your research is positioned in the context of what has already been examined and understood in your particular area of interest.

Introduction

By this stage you will have identified the focus area of your research and may have a good idea of your key research question or questions. You have begun to think about the kinds of information which will help you find out more about the issues you are interested in. It may be tempting to skip over this section to get to the 'real' research stuff in the following three chapters, but that could be a serious mistake. Understanding what other researchers have found that relates to your area of interest, how they have approached their research and how they have interpreted their findings is an important part of any new research study. It enables you to position yourself in the debate around the issues that interest you and to make your own contribution.

> *Research tells a story and the existing literature helps us identify where we are in the story currently. It is up to those writing (a research study) to continue that story with new research and new perspectives but they must first be familiar with the story before they can move forward.*

(Wortman, 2013, unpaged)

What is a literature review?

The literature review section of a research study fulfils a number of purposes, each of which is important in its own right.

- It sets the context of the new research study by indicating what has already been investigated.

- It indicates how the new research fits into this body of knowledge.

- It opens up the significant debates associated with the focus of the research.

- It prevents unknowing duplication of previous research, although you may deliberately choose to replicate a previous study in a different context.

- It helps to identify the different research approaches used within your area of interest.

- It identifies gaps in existing knowledge, which your new research may help to fill.

As you can see, carrying out a literature review may mean that you make some changes to your initial research questions and/or your intended methods of data collection. The processes of reading around your area of interest, and refining your research question and research approach go hand in hand.

What does a good literature review look like?

First, your discussion of existing research and other literature should be as relevant to your chosen focus area and your main research questions as possible. While it is unlikely you will find research or educational writing which is *exactly* about your research question (else why are you carrying out your study?), you do need to be able to place your work within the context of other research and ideas.

Equally importantly, your discussion needs to engage with the key ideas or themes that are discussed in the literature related to your focus area. This is sometimes referred to as 'the field' of your research, so that your literature review 'maps the field'. Engaging with these key ideas means much more than merely describing what other people say or have found. A good literature review is not a list of who said what, but a critical and analytical discussion of similarities and differences between different writers and researchers. This helps the reader understand how and why your research study will add to the existing field of knowledge in your chosen focus area.

Finally, your literature review needs to lead the reader towards the particular research questions which you intend to investigate. This is sometimes referred to as 'funnelling down', so that your discussion starts with the wider issues associated with your chosen focus area, and then narrows down to the more specific issues in which you are interested.

How much literature you include, and how long your literature review is, depends on the way in which you are expected to write up your research. If you are writing a longer study, such as a Master's dissertation, then the literature review will be expected to be proportionately longer and to cover a wider range of issues relating to your chosen area of interest than if you are writing a shorter report or assignment.

What kind of literature should we be looking for?

Your literature review must be based on authoritative sources. By this we usually mean literature that is based on good evidence and/or theoretical principles which have been endorsed by other experts in the field. Articles in peer-reviewed academic journals fall into this category, as do books published by educational publishers, whereas much of the material found freely available on the Internet may not. You may also need to refer to other kinds of documents, such as policy documents, which are not subject to peer review in the same way as educational texts or research articles, but which may be important to the context of your study.

Poulson and Wallace (2004) list four main types of literature associated with educational writing, and your literature review could include examples from the first three categories:

- theoretical literature;

- research literature;

- policy literature;

- practice literature.

The last category of 'practice literature', including material such as teaching guides, lesson ideas etc., is not generally included in a literature review. Many practice texts do not include references to academic sources, even though the underpinning ideas are usually indirectly based on educational theory or research evidence. Similarly, you should avoid using many references to educational textbooks. Although these will make use of academic references to support key points, they are what are known as secondary sources, and you should be reading and referring to the original materials (the primary sources) wherever possible. Thomas (2009, pp31–4) discusses primary and secondary sources further and provides a helpful table, which identifies the advantages and disadvantages of different kinds of literature.

Wikipedia should be used with extreme caution. Given its scope, it can provide information about a brand new area, and it can be a helpful stepping stone, but the entries vary in quality and authority. You should always be able to locate a more reliable source of evidence for the point you want to make.

Finding the relevant literature

If you are studying at university, you may have been given suggested reading lists or recommended articles which might give you a start, but you will need to do most of your searching independently. Whatever you are going to look for first, whether it is a book, an article or a government document, your search is almost certainly going to start online. In order to make your search as efficient and effective as possible, there are several key strategies you may need to employ.

The first, and most obvious one, is to identify your search terms, although this can sometimes be trickier than you might think. The following example illustrates some of the strategies you might need to use in order to locate relevant and recent literature on a particular topic.

Imagine that you have decided to conduct some research around 'the effects of ability grouping on pupil attainment in primary schools'. Perhaps you are interested in a particular subject area, or on the impact of ability grouping on pupils' motivation or self-esteem. Initially, you want to know what kind of research has been conducted around ability grouping and what the main debates have been about. Entering 'ability grouping primary schools' into Google™ returns more than 210,000 results (Figure 4.1).

Clearly, you are not going to check all these results, but you already know that Google™ prioritises certain sites in terms of popularity and relevance, so checking the first few pages is likely to be sufficient. There is a heading for 'scholarly articles' at the top of the page, but two of the three articles identified refer to secondary schools, so you decide to leave that for the moment. As you look down the first three results there seem to be some interesting possibilities, including some articles, but the publication dates of these all seem to be at least ten years old. There is a research news item from a UK university dated 2013 which looks as if it might be relevant, and there is also a newspaper item from 2012 reporting on an OECD study about ability grouping. Both of these are summaries of the research findings and are therefore secondary sources. You will need to locate the original research reports in order to find out about the details.

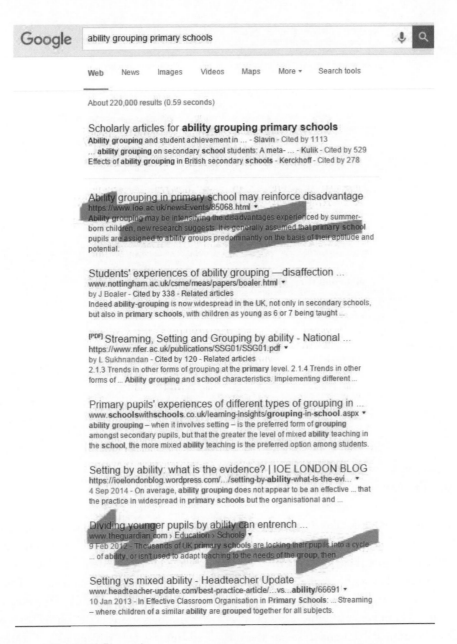

Figure 4.1 Initial Google™ search

You note down the details you can find in order to try to search for these later. You have noticed that the same names have come up several times as authors of research articles, so you note these down too. You can search for other articles by these authors using Google Scholar™.

You have also noticed a link at the bottom of the page to a 'literature review' on the effects of pupil grouping (Figure 4.2).

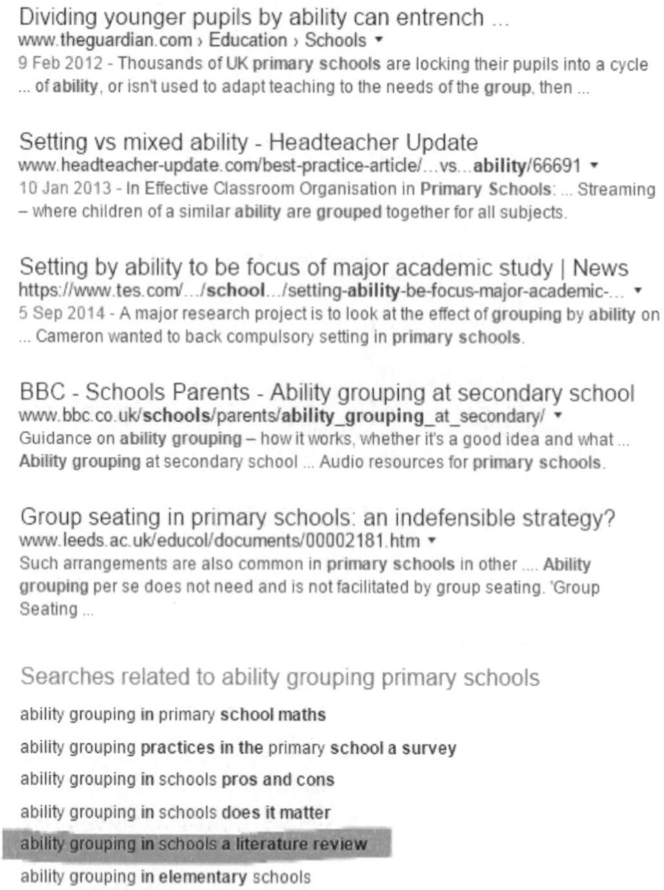

Dividing younger pupils by ability can entrench ...
www.theguardian.com › Education › Schools ▾
9 Feb 2012 - Thousands of UK primary schools are locking their pupils into a cycle
... of ability, or isn't used to adapt teaching to the needs of the group, then ...

Setting vs mixed ability - Headteacher Update
www.headteacher-update.com/best-practice-article/...vs...ability/66691 ▾
10 Jan 2013 - In Effective Classroom Organisation in Primary Schools: ... Streaming
– where children of a similar ability are grouped together for all subjects.

Setting by ability to be focus of major academic study | News
https://www.tes.com/.../school.../setting-ability-be-focus-major-academic-... ▾
5 Sep 2014 - A major research project is to look at the effect of grouping by ability on
... Cameron wanted to back compulsory setting in primary schools.

BBC - Schools Parents - Ability grouping at secondary school
www.bbc.co.uk/schools/parents/ability_grouping_at_secondary/ ▾
Guidance on ability grouping – how it works, whether it's a good idea and what ...
Ability grouping at secondary school ... Audio resources for primary schools.

Group seating in primary schools: an indefensible strategy?
www.leeds.ac.uk/educol/documents/00002181.htm ▾
Such arrangements are also common in primary schools in other .... Ability
grouping per se does not need and is not facilitated by group seating. 'Group
Seating ...

Searches related to ability grouping primary schools

ability grouping in primary school maths

ability grouping practices in the primary school a survey

ability grouping in schools pros and cons

ability grouping in schools does it matter

ability grouping in schools a literature review

ability grouping in elementary schools

Figure 4.2 Related searches

Clicking on the link takes you to more search results. The top review on this new list is dated 2005, but it is still a good find, since it will provide a good overview of research conducted before then, and may help to identify some of the key debates. There are also links to searches with terms such as 'ability grouping in schools pros and cons'. These look like exactly what you are looking for, but when you follow the links they take you to a number of personal blog pages or to websites run by various organisations. These provide summary statements about the various advantages or disadvantages of ability grouping, but few of them contain any academic references to support their key points. There is no way to check the information in these websites, so they are best ignored, although you may want to make a list of the key arguments in case you can find better sources of evidence to support them.

Searching Google™ seems to have taken you as far as you can go at present, so you turn to Google Scholar™ as a reliable source of academic resources. Using the same search term as before, you find a number of results, but most are still dated around 2003–2004 (Figure 4.3). Surely there has been further research into ability grouping since then? You try restricting your search to material published since 2011 by clicking on the

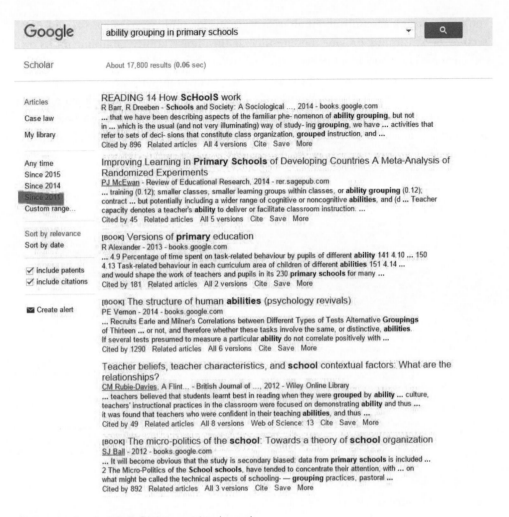

Figure 4.3 Google Scholar™ date-restricted search

link on the left-hand side of the page, and several articles about inclusive practice in classrooms come up, but they aren't quite what you are looking for. You need to refine your search term further.

Improving your search strategies

Up to now you have been using what has been called the 'low-hanging fruit' search strategy (Thomas, 2009; Ford, 2012). This means using search engines such as Google™ or Google Scholar™ with a single search term and seeing what crops up. As we have discovered, although we have found one or two useful items, this strategy has not enabled you to locate the most recent research literature on your focus area. You will need to employ a more systematic approach and narrow down your search field by using more advanced search tools and more carefully chosen terms.

You need to think carefully about alternative terms for 'ability grouping'. Would 'setting' or 'streaming' provide more results? Is the phrase 'ability grouping' on its own sufficient? Could you add a further term such as 'attainment'? Thinking back to your initial research area, this is one of the aspects you want to investigate, so it should be included in your search. Using the Advanced Search option on the drop-down menu in the search bar in Google Scholar™, you try searching for any articles published since 2000 containing the exact phrase 'ability grouping' and with the word 'attainment' as at least one of the other words in the whole article (Figure 4.4).

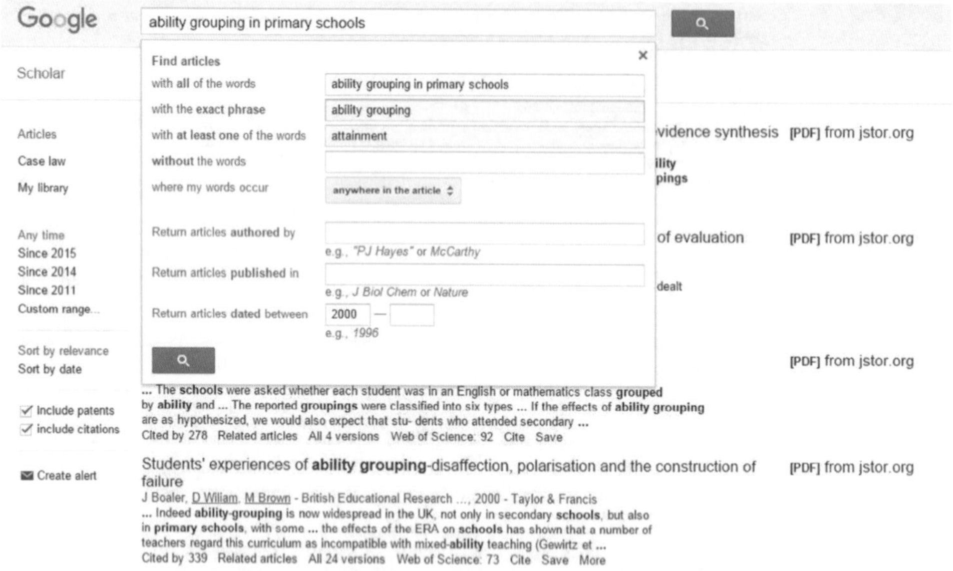

Figure 4.4 Advanced Google Scholar™ search

This time your search is more successful. You find references for a couple of recent articles by one of the key authors you noted previously, plus a pre-publication version of the research referred to in the university research summary you found on Google™. Now you have the details of these research articles you can either locate them using your university's on-line journal subscription (Figure 4.5), or request them via inter-library loan if your library does not subscribe to the relevant journals. While you are on the journal website, don't forget to look at the box on the right hand of the article page headed 'users also read'. This will link you to other articles that could be of interest. You should also look at the key words given below the abstract, as comparing these with your own search terms may help you find further information.

Another way you can use Google Scholar™ is to use the 'citation link' on a reference to an earlier research article (Figure 4.6). This will tell you how many people have referred to this article since publication. Clicking on the link will give you details of these various articles, so that in this way you can search forward in time from an

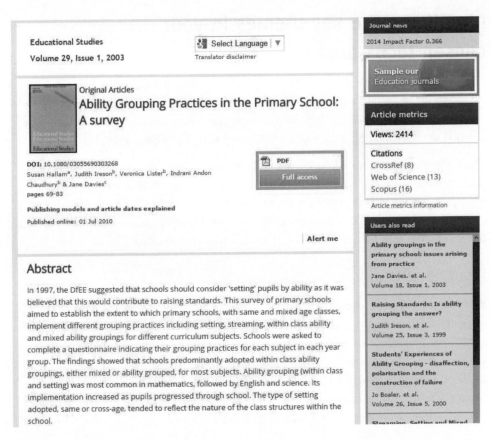

Abstract

In 1997, the DfEE suggested that schools should consider 'setting' pupils by ability as it was believed that this would contribute to raising standards. This survey of primary schools aimed to establish the extent to which primary schools, with same and mixed age classes, implement different grouping practices including setting, streaming, within class ability and mixed ability groupings for different curriculum subjects. Schools were asked to complete a questionnaire indicating their grouping practices for each subject in each year group. The findings showed that schools predominantly adopted within class ability groupings, either mixed or ability grouped, for most subjects. Ability grouping (within class and setting) was most common in mathematics, followed by English and science. Its implementation increased as pupils progressed through school. The type of setting adopted, same or cross-age, tended to reflect the nature of the class structures within the school.

Figure 4.5 Journal article

older source. In this case, clicking on the citation link for a reference dated 2003 brings up 37 other references, some of which are fairly recent, although not all are relevant to your key research focus.

Google Scholar™ is not infallible and there may be research articles and other scholarly material available which are not available via this search tool, although the advantage of Scholar is that it is freely available to everyone. Your university library will probably subscribe to other academic search tools such as SciVerse Scopus or Web of Science, and these may bring up other items if you use their advanced search facilities. Your university librarians will be able to help you to make the most of these tools, which are not available to the general public. Alternatively, you could use a good reference text such as Ford (2012) to give you further help.

Ability grouping practices in the **primary school**: A survey   [PDF] from tandfonline.com
S Hallam, J Ireson, V Lister, IA Chaudhury... - Educational ..., 2003 - Taylor & Francis
... **Schools** were asked to complete a questionnaire indicating their **grouping** practices for each ...
predominantly adopted within class **ability groupings**, either mixed or **ability grouped**, for most ...
Ability grouping (within class and setting) was most common in mathematics, followed by ...
Cited by 37 Related articles All 9 versions Web of Science: 13 Cite Save More

Figure 4.6 Further references

Identifying the key themes in your chosen focus area

Earlier in this chapter we mentioned the importance of identifying the key themes or 'big ideas' in the literature related to your focus area. This requires you to compare and/or contrast ideas and research findings from different authors and to discuss these connections, rather than merely stating what various writers say without linking their ideas.

There are several strategies you can use to help you to organise your thinking here, once you feel you have located a range of literature sources. Which strategy or strategies you use will depend on your preferred way of working – there is no single 'right' way to approach this important stage of developing your literature review. What is important is that you adopt a critical approach to your reading.

Reading critically

By saying that you need to adopt a critical approach, we mean that you should think carefully about what the author is saying and the evidence that is used to support their argument. This is not the same as 'criticising' their work in terms of saying what is wrong with it. As we have already indicated, the literature we expect you to be reading has been subject to expert review before being published, so critical reading is not a matter of fault finding or disagreeing, but one of evaluating the claims that are made in the light of the evidence presented.

You may also need to engage in some 'reading between the lines' in order to determine the values, beliefs and/or assumptions made by the author, which might affect the ways in which they interpret their findings or argue their point of view. This is not to suggest that holding such views is in any way wrong. Most educational writers and researchers acknowledge that being 'objective' is actually impossible and instead aim to make their own particular theoretical or ideological framework clear to the reader.

Example from practice

To illustrate the ways in which reading can be both analytical and critical, we have selected a paragraph from an article by Hallam and Parsons (2013), which examines evidence on the current use of ability grouped sets in primary schools. You are advised to access the full article, in order to view this paragraph in context.

The introduction to the article has set out the main arguments for and against the use of setting by ability, supported by reference to a wide range of research. The literature review first considers the historical situation with regard to ability grouping in primary schools and then discusses whether setting affects attainment. Following a paragraph outlining some evidence from the USA, the article continues as follows.

In the UK, there is limited evidence about the effects of setting at primary level. School self reports suggest that the effects are mixed (Hallam, Ireson, and Davies 2004b), while

> Whitburn (2001) studying the progress of over 1000 pupils at Key Stage 2 in mathematics found that when the same teaching materials were used the test results of pupils in mixed ability classes were significantly better than those taught in sets. Mixed ability classes benefited the less able pupils but attainment of the more able did not suffer. In case studies of 12 primary schools, Kutnick et al. (2006) found that where setting was adopted performance was rarely better at KS2 than local and national averages and value added was generally negative.
>
> (Hallam and Parsons, 2013, p395)

If we analyse this paragraph in detail, we can see how the authors have constructed their argument.

In the UK, there is limited evidence about the effects of setting at primary level.	The first sentence alerts us to the fact there is limited evidence from research in the UK, as a comparison with evidence from the USA. This acts as a cautionary warning about the extent of the evidence presented in the rest of the paragraph, although it does not suggest it is unreliable. This first sentence also indicates the key focus of the paragraph.
School self-reports suggest that the effects are mixed (Hallam, Ireson, and Davies 2004b), while Whitburn (2001) studying the progress of over 1,000 pupils at Key Stage 2 in mathematics found that when the same teaching materials were used the test results of pupils in mixed ability classes were significantly better than those taught in sets.	This long sentence includes reference to two different research studies about the effects of ability grouping on attainment in primary schools. The first study is based on school 'self-reports' and seems to be inconclusive, whereas the second study seems to have clearer outcomes. Notice the use of the word 'while' linking the two studies. Used in this way, it emphasises the contrast between the 'mixed' outcomes of the first study and the apparently conclusive results of the second. What would the effect have been if reference to the two studies had been reversed?
Mixed ability classes benefited the less able pupils but attainment of the more able did not suffer.	This sentence adds findings from the second research study and specifically addresses a common argument against mixed ability grouping – that more able pupils do less well.
In case studies of 12 primary schools, Kutnick et al. (2006) found that where setting was adopted, performance was rarely better at KS2 than local and national averages and value added was generally negative.	This final sentence in the paragraph refers to a further study, of a different type, as additional evidence that ability grouping does not substantially improve pupils' performance at Key Stage 2.
Overall, the 'flow' of argument in this paragraph leads the reader towards the conclusion that setting by ability in primary schools in the UK does not improve pupil attainment. As readers, we need to ask ourselves if this represents the beliefs of the authors and, if so, how might this affect the rest of the article?	

For a further example of analysis of a section of a literature review, see Bryan et al. (2010), p151.

Adopting a sceptical stance

Although the argument in this paragraph seems fairly convincing, there are some further questions you might wish to ask. Although we know quite a bit about the research by Whitburn (2001) – that it involved progress in mathematics for 1,000 pupils and that the same teaching materials were used for all pupils – we know very little about the 'mixed' results from the study based on school self-reports. How many schools were involved and what kinds of questions were asked? How far are these two research studies really comparing like with like, even though they are included in the same sentence? Similarly, you may wish to know more about the case study research mentioned in the final sentence.

Although you cannot continue to check back on other research studies indefinitely, it is important to maintain this kind of questioning outlook on your reading as you prepare your own literature review. Even with research published in well-respected, peer-reviewed journals, critical questions can, and should, still be asked.

How do you prefer to read academic material?

Are you a note-taker?

While the act of note-taking can be helpful in clarifying your understanding, it can also be counterproductive. Most of us learned our note-taking skills at secondary school, where the emphasis is often on noting down facts. This approach is not always helpful in terms of supporting critical reading, where the emphasis is more on understanding and evaluating the arguments presented. Note-taking approaches which tend towards summarising your reading rather than analysing what you read can contribute to the production of poor quality literature reviews in the form of lists of unrelated summaries of writing: 'Jones ( ) says this. Smith ( ) says that'.

If you find it challenging to follow the arguments in a longer piece of writing the first time you read it, you could try noting the key ideas or arguments in each section or even each paragraph. Sometimes you can even cut and paste these from the text. You should end up with an outline of the argument that author/s intend to make to help your understanding, so that you can see the 'big picture' of the writing, including the key themes.

You may want to consider using a standardised format for your note-taking so that you can make connections between the items you read. Poulson and Wallace (2004) offer a very detailed format, which you could adapt to suit your own requirements, or you could use something like the simplified format offered at the end of this chapter. An article by Campbell (2013) has been used as an example. Taber (2013, pp17–18) offers further resources.

Do you annotate or underline parts of the text as you read?

This strategy avoids the problems associated with simple summarising, but too much underlining or highlighting can make it hard to identify key issues. In order to know when highlighting or underlining is going to be helpful to you later, you need to have an idea of the big picture of what you are reading first. Our advice is that you should read the whole article or chapter through at least once *without making any marks at all.* Some people also advise using pencil to begin with, once you start annotating, so that you can still change your mind.

You need to remind yourself why you are annotating the text – you want to identify key arguments and their supporting evidence, but you also want to be able to ask questions about the conclusions drawn by the author/s. Longer comments or questions may require the use of sticky notes or additional notes. If you are reading electronically, there may be ways in which you can directly link your notes to your reading. You may want to indicate connections with other literature, using marginal notes, or you may prefer to use a standardised format as above, once you are satisfied you have completed your reading.

Organising your ideas to structure your review

Your literature review is often referred to as a 'story', because it should have a clear narrative centred on the key ideas in your focus area. Earlier on in this chapter we also talked about the need for your review to 'funnel down' towards your own research question (which may have been modified through your reading). You might like to look at the progression of ideas in the article by Campbell (2013) referred to above, to see how the order of ideas in the literature review moves from the more general topic of children's birth month related to attainment, towards the specific areas of in-class ability grouping and teacher perceptions in which she is particularly interested.

It can be helpful to develop a visual summary such as a concept map or spider diagram to organise your ideas. Alternatively, develop a chart, in which each key theme or idea is identified, along with supporting references and some chosen quotations. Where there are different views or conflicting evidence associated with a theme, this also needs to be indicated.

Example from practice

The section of the literature review from Hallam and Parsons (2013) referred to above might look like the table below.

Section heading: Does setting affect attainment in the primary school?

Positive impact on all pupils	Slavin 1987 USA	Improvement for all pupils with regrouping across age levels
Positive impact on some pupils	Kulik & Kulik 1992 USA	Benefits for higher achieving pupils, no adverse effects for others with cross-age grouping
	Whitburn 2001 UK	
	Fuchs et al. 1998 USA	Benefits for lower ability, no adverse effects for higher in mixed ability mathematics
	Webb, Welner & Zuinga 2001 USA	Within class ability grouping beneficial for middle & higher ability. NB neutral or negative for lower ability
	Lichevski & Kutscher 1998 USA	Mixed ability grouping benefited low & middle ability but high ability did not suffer

(Continued)

(Continued)

Negative impact on some pupils	Kutnick et al. 2006 UK	Value added generally negative at KS 2 where <u>setting</u> used. No significant improvement over national averages
No significant impact on pupils	Hallam, Ireson & Davies 2004 UK	School self-reports on <u>setting</u> – mixed outcomes
Other considerations	Webb, Welner & Zuinga 2001 Leonard 2001	Group functioning also important Mixed ability groups generally better for group work

Note that the underlined phrases emphasise the different types of ability grouping considered in the research studies – an important consideration in comparing the studies. Hallam and Parsons (2013) have structured this section of their review to reflect differences between the USA and UK, and also differences in types of ability grouping.

Putting your ideas together

When you have read sufficiently widely to have identified the key ideas in your chosen area, and you are familiar with the different perspectives or arguments presented by writers and researchers, you are ready to write! At the start of this chapter we introduced the idea of research as a continuing story, where the literature review tells 'the story so far . . .' and your own research study becomes the next episode.

Your introduction should aim to engage the reader. Why is the general area of your research regarded as important to others? Why is it important to you? Are there controversial issues associated with your focus area? Has your reading identified gaps in knowledge that your own research might be aiming to fill?

Early on in your review, you should explore any key terms from research and make it clear how you intend to use these in your own work. For example, in the research studies we have used in this chapter, 'ability grouping' could be used to apply to 'setting by ability across two or more classes', 'cross-age' ability grouping or to 'within-class' ability grouping. If you were intending to research the use of ability grouping in a primary school, it would be very important to be clear about which kind you meant.

Now you write about each of the key themes or ideas you have identified in your reading. Ideally, each paragraph should connect ideas from several sources, either to show similarities or conflicting evidence. Look again at the extract from Hallam and Parsons (2013) for an example. Aim to move from more general ideas towards those that are particularly relevant to your own research study, as in the example by Campbell (2013). Use subheadings where you feel they will help the reader, but also look for ways to connect the ideas in different paragraphs. This will be discussed in more detail in a later chapter in this book.

Unlike other kinds of essay, the concluding section of your literature review will not attempt to draw all the ideas together, but it will focus towards the key question your research is attempting to answer. The literature review is not so much a complete story, but more of a cliff-hanger.

So you think it's all over?

The relationship between your literature review and your research study is recursive. As you write the section of your assignment which discusses the findings of your research, you will be expected to make links back to the literature you discussed in the review section. It is not unusual for you to find things that were unexpected as a result of your research, which you also want to connect with existing research literature or educational theory.

If you did not include discussion on this new theme in your literature review the first time, it is good practice to revise the review, to ensure it is included. You may find that you want to rewrite the introduction in order to emphasise this new aspect which has emerged from your own research. Doing research is often full of surprises!

Things to think about

1. Through your literature review have you explored key ideas and placed your work in a context?

2. Does your literature review bring different ideas about your topic together in a discussion, rather than being a disconnected list?

3. Does your literature review draw mainly upon literature that has been subject to review by experts before publication? Have you used primary sources wherever possible?

4. Have you used specialised academic search engines, experimenting with various key words in your search terms to get the best results from the Internet?

5. Have you asked critical questions of the literature you have read? Have you asked yourself 'Why is the writer saying this?' and 'How well have they justified their conclusions?'.

6. Do your notes and annotations help you identify key ideas and evidence that you can compare with other reading?

7. Have you worked out the different ways in which key ideas from your reading can be organised in order to support the argument *you* want to make?

8. Is your literature review structured to engage the reader and enable them to see the connections between the key themes which inform your own research?

References

Bryan, H, Carpenter, C and Hoult, S (2010) *Learning and Teaching at M Level: A Guide for Student Teachers*. London: SAGE.

Campbell, T (2013) Stratified at seven: In-class ability-grouping and the relative age effect. *British Educational Research Journal*, 40(5): 749–71.

Ford, N (2012) *The Essential Guide to Using the Web for Research*. London: SAGE.

Hallam, S and Parsons, S (2013) The incidence and make up of ability grouped sets in the UK primary school. *Research Papers in Education*, 28(4): 393–420.

Poulson, L and Wallace, M (2004) *Learning to Read Critically in Teaching and Learning*. London: SAGE.

Taber, KS (2013) *Classroom-based Research and Evidence-based Practice: An Introduction*. London: SAGE.

Thomas, G (2009) *How to do your Research Project*. London: SAGE.

Wortman, S (2013) The Literature Review: For Dissertations: Research Guides. Available at: http://guides.lib.umich.edu/c.php?g=283139&p=1886326 (accessed July 2015).

Further reading

Cottrell, S (2005) *Critical Thinking Skills: Developing Effective Analysis and Argument*. London: Palgrave.

Fairbarn, G and Fairbarn, S (2001) *Reading at University: A Guide for Students*. Buckingham: Open University Press.

Ford, N (2012) *The Essential Guide to Using the Web for Research*. London: SAGE.

Holliday, A (2007) *Doing and Writing Qualitative Research* (2nd edn). London: SAGE.

Walford, G (1991) *Doing Educational Research*. London: Routledge.

Wallace, M and Wray, A (2006) *Critical Reading and Writing for Postgraduates*. London: SAGE.

Chapter 5

Methodology: what approach should I take?

Gill Hope

Objectives

This chapter:

- develops your awareness and understanding of methodology literature;
- enables you to give a clear explanation of what kind of data you will collect and how;
- ensures you are able to take ethical issues surrounding your research into account.

Chapter summary

Getting the right data is at the heart of a successful research project – you cannot find out what you want to know unless you have collected data which answers your question.

Introduction

A good methodology justifies your research design – why you approached the research as you did. You need to be able to relate your design choices to your aims and demonstrate that your choices form the best strategy for answering your research question. Your methodology summarises all the things you need to think about *before* you begin to plan your data gathering as follows.

- Demonstrating that you understand the theoretical underpinning of doing research in the classroom.

- Explaining the kind of data you want to gather; why you believe this will be the best way to answer your research question.

- Making explicit any assumptions that you may have based on prior knowledge, understanding, observations or personal beliefs/opinions.

- Showing that you have considered the moral, ethical (and possibly political) implications of what you are doing.

Your methodology section will probably be expected to be approximately a quarter of the total length of the assignment, so it bears a significant portion of the marks you will receive. It is how you explain to your reader why and how you did what you did so that they can follow the logical steps you took to plan and execute your research. In order to choose the right research strategy, you need to know which choices would be most relevant in answering your research question, plus you need to know how to gather the type of data you believe will do that best. This chapter will help you understand those choices.

What is a methodology?

Research is about the pursuit of knowledge, finding out something for yourself by making sense of the world around you in a creative and insightful way. Your research question contains the germs of your ideas, refined through your reading and honed through your literature review. Your methodology is the statement of intent; how you intend to go about answering your research question. You are not sure at the moment quite where that journey may lead, but you have gained some knowledge of what is already known and some thoughts on how you might proceed.

In order to demonstrate an appropriate depth of critical analysis and insight to create a sound research framework, you need to show a good understanding of why you are doing what you are doing. Choice of methodology will influence (maybe even dictate) choice of data collection methods and analysis techniques, but a mere description of these does not make a methodology, however appropriate they may be to investigating the research question. Choices need to be made on the basis of fitness for purpose: what can be collected efficiently in the time available in the context to which you have access? You might enjoy number crunching on Excel™ and producing charts, but if your research question cannot be answered that way, then you will have to choose another path.

What you see, especially in a social situation such as a classroom, is filtered through the lens of your own viewpoint (physical, emotional, cultural, intellectual, religious, and so on). You cannot say things such as 'I know that was what was happening because I saw it with my own eyes'. Your eyes, unfortunately, are not unbiased. The theory of what can be *known* is called epistemology, but bold claims to knowledge of what *is* should be avoided because there are so many ways of perceiving social reality (or 'truth').

Social situations, said Rittel and Webber (1976), are 'wicked problems' (called 'fuzzy problems' by other writers) whose answers are unclear, 'indeterminate' (not true/false or good/bad, but better/worse or 'satisfying' or 'good enough') (p275), and therefore lack 'one right answer'. Solutions may be chosen from several equally valid possibilities; they may be capable of change or improvement later; or the sample size may be too small to claim generalisability. Rittel and Webber comment: *The information needed to* understand *the problem depends on one's idea for* solving *it*. (op cit., p273).

Research paradigms: what are the theories from which to choose?

Think of the word 'paradigm' as meaning 'theoretical framework' – you are choosing a way of approaching your research according to theories of how we can make sense of and 'know' the world around us. From a scientific perspective, this is often done by doing 'experiments' which measure physical attributes and draw conclusions from 'hard', numerical data. This doesn't really work when you are researching social contexts where what can be measured or counted is less obvious. Bruner (1986) distinguished between *two ways of knowing* (scientific and narrative) that relate to two different ways of asking and answering questions. In making this distinction, Bruner was not suggesting that one was better than the other; each simply aims at a different kind of truthfulness. To these are linked the two kinds of data you can collect in researching: *quantitative* and *qualitative*.

- Scientific ways of seeking 'truth' > positivist / empiricist research methods > quantitative data (= quantities, i.e. numbers).

- Narrative ways of seeing the world, 'truth-likeness' > interpretative methods > qualitative data (= qualities, described in words, pictures or sounds).

Note: The words 'quantitative' and 'qualitative' describe data. They do *not* describe a methodology or a research paradigm. So do not say 'I am using a qualitative methodology'; rather say 'I am collecting qualitative data'.

You can combine both methods in one study. This is called 'pragmatism' (as in being pragmatic and choosing to use whatever works best) and employs 'mixed methods'. So, for instance, you could do a quantitative overview – perhaps giving out a questionnaire to find out how many hours children spend on extra-curricular sport and then zoom in one child or group of children to interview according to their answers. Alternatively, you could spend time in a classroom observing what happens, analyse your observations and turn them into numbers which can be plotted as graphs or represented in other numerical forms; then you spend time in another setting and see if the same pattern emerges.

The advantages of doing both are:

- It could lead to your conclusions being on a much firmer footing – you have looked in two different ways.

- Quantitative data alone doesn't provide the 'why?'; qualitative data alone can be accused of subjectivity – i.e. to represent your own bias and interpretation.

- Some phenomena and/or research questions do not clearly fall into one camp but suggest that both would be appropriate.

The advantages to choosing just one are:

- Personal preference: you might feel that only quantitative data really 'proves' anything or, conversely, that you feel more confident with words rather than numbers.

- It makes the study 'simpler' just to do one and you could collect two or more data types within either (e.g. action research plus a case study).

- The data you are examining exists in numerical form already.

- Your sample size is too small to sensibly assert that quantitative data would be meaningful.

- The issue/question you are investigating clearly lends itself to one or the other.

The reasons for your choice must derive from the question you are investigating. You need to be able to say 'I am investigating such and such, therefore I am choosing such a methodology because . . . ' However, you do not need to make all the decisions before you start.

Example from practice

In my own research into young children using drawing for designing, there was one child, Zara, who always did something completely different and unexpected. Her response not only challenged the adequacy of my quantitative analysis instrument but also what I believed creativity to be.

I thought my quantitative approach would enable me to see the relationship between the design drawing and the final product (Figure 5.1). It was child centred and focused on what I believed to be the essence of being able to use drawing for designing: understanding of purpose. From this emanated eight axes ('Dimensions of design drawing') and each child's drawing and final product were scored on these 5-point scales to produce a radial plot for each child's development across the project.

For every task, Zara got top scores for 'Generating and Developing Ideas' but for 'Exploring the Possibilities of the Task' and 'Addressing the Constraints of the Task' she consistently scored low.

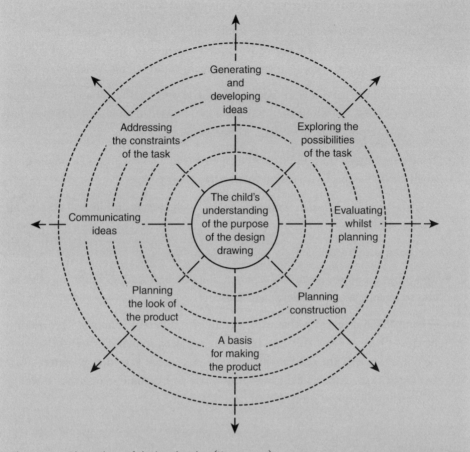

Figure 5.1 Dimensions of design drawing (Hope, 2003)

However innovative her ideas, they consistently failed to address the task criteria. Was she highly creative or just plain off-task? Was 'creativity' different according to circumstances?

The quantitative instrument allowed me to easily see the mismatch, but the questions it raised pushed me into much deeper theoretical thinking than I had bargained for.

Triangulation

This term is taken from map-making, in which a view of the same landscape is mapped from different vantage points, which neatly describes the essence of its value. These different viewpoints might be:

1. 'Within method' (same method different contexts).

    • Collecting data at different times, places or from/about different people or groups of people.

    • Using different Investigators (perhaps asking someone else to look at that video).

2. Or 'between methods' (different methods applied to same context).

- Distributing questionnaires to the whole staff and then interviewing key respondents (but be aware that giving questionnaires to the whole staff and then interviewing just the senior management team could be misconstrued).

- Questionnaires that allow for both quantitative and qualitative analysis – e.g. a mix of 'tickbox' questions that may be yes/no or graded on a scale and questions that allow respondents to explain or express opinions.

- Time sampling to track children's engagement in a lesson and then holding small group feedback discussion to ascertain their perspective

- Assess all children's maths work on one day > choose six children to observe for process skills.

3. Or 'between paradigms'.

- You could examine one child's experience of school from a social perspective and also from an academic achievement perspective.

- A comparison of settings that exist within very different contexts. This might be cross-phase or cross-cultural. However, you need to be very careful that you do not imply that the one in which you place yourself is somehow 'better'. Aim to use the experience reflexively to illuminate and become more aware of your own assumptions and preconceptions.

Example from practice

Yasmin and Anna went to East Africa for their alternative professional placement, during which they were expected to conduct some research. They had each formulated some research questions based on their expectations of rural Africa: large classes, limited resources, formal methods, no differentiation and little creativity. They discovered that despite the large classes and limited resources, the teachers cared about every child and knew their families. Parents with the finances to do so would choose strategically which child (often the oldest boy) would be sent to a private school. This did not mean that the rest of the children were not motivated to learn. They expected to work hard and help each other. Their expectations of schooling were that the teacher instructed them and they learnt. They did not enjoy the more 'creative' approaches that Yasmin and Anna tried to introduce in small groups, even asking to return to class so that they could learn their lessons.

Anna continued with her idea of comparing the children's clothing (as proxy for economic status) with their educational achievement. The teachers' knowledge of the pattern of passing clothing down through families meant that no stigma was attached to worn-out clothes or lack of shoes – and the children were expected to do just as well as their older siblings.

Yasmin, on the other hand, scrapped her original research ideas altogether. She prepared a questionnaire related to the challenges of their observations to their preconceptions and, on return, she presented this to the rest of her student group. Her analysis centred on the mismatch between their peers' preconceptions and what the two of them had observed, and the implications for teaching children in the UK about life in Africa.

Positivism/empiricism

This is Bruner's 'scientific' way of knowing.

- Asserts that the only means of knowledge is through our physical senses.

- Begins from a hypothesis to be tested.

- Designs and carries out research tasks/experiments to test the hypothesis.

- Data is usually quantitative (i.e. numerical) and analysed using arithmetical or statistical techniques.

- Results are expressed numerically and used to prove/disprove the hypothesis.

- The aim of positivist research is creating a theory that can be applied in a wide range of situations: 'generalisability'.

Example from practice

Lorna used her school data to investigate whether or not 'pupil premium' payments were an effective means of targeting children who might be at risk of not achieving their academic potential on the basis of low parental income. This allowed her to analyse data that would have been impossible to collect first hand.

One pattern that emerged was that it was not necessarily the children from the lowest income group who underachieved. In fact, many of these children did relatively better than their more affluent peers from a similar social background. Were low-income parents seeing education as a way out of poverty for their children, Lorna wondered, or did the slightly more affluent parents not have the time to spend with their children because they were both working?

Although the numbers of children of families who were recent immigrants to the UK were small in her sample, these children were likely to be achieving well after two years in school, regardless of the family's current circumstances, thus highlighting the difference between economic and social capital.

Analysing the school data caused Lorna to reflect on the possibility that parental educational levels, aspirations and motivation to help their children towards a better life might be the real factors involved. While recognising the limited capability of large-scale quantitative data to tell the whole story when dealing with complex and detailed social issues, she asserted its usefulness in identifying the weakness of the simple link between economic disadvantage and low educational achievement.

Your research, too, might reveal new insights and relationships within your school's data that had not been seen before because no one had asked your question. This might be extremely useful to your school.

The aim of collecting *quantitative data* is to prove something mathematically, perhaps to demonstrate its frequency. However, it is easy to be beguiled into thinking that the 'figures speak for themselves' and that numbers, charts and graphs do not need judicial rpretation. They can be manipulated! Think of the shock headlines '20 per cent of ...dren cannot yet . . . ' compared to '80 per cent of our children achieved . . . '

It can be difficult to argue conclusively that certain trends exist without some numbers to back up your claims, but numbers alone may not provide the depth of analysis necessary for drawing conclusions about educational issues. You need to attempt to find out *why*.

Turning qualitative data into quantitative data can establish trends and help to counter personal biases and interests. I found this in my own research. It was all too easy to assume that many children were using drawing for designing effectively just because I noticed every time they did. Trying to find a good number of examples proved more elusive. I had to collect all the drawings, analyse them and do rather a lot of number crunching. However, eventually I got to the stage of not only knowing what the children could do at different ages, but also how to help them use their drawings more effectively to develop their design ideas.

Quantitative methods are often more suitable for large-scale research such as national trends than for providing insight into a single instance, whether this be one child, one class or one school. Despite the quantity of numerical data with which educationalists are surrounded, they tell us little about specific circumstances, let alone individuals. This does not mean that quantifying your data is totally inappropriate for small-scale research. You do not necessarily need to decide your analysis categories in advance as you can easily add extra columns on a spreadsheet as you analyse your observations and see what has emerged. (This is very useful for turning qualitative data into quantitative data.) Start with a blank spreadsheet and add a new column every time something new turns up while adding an extra cell each time an existing category occurs.

However, beware making mathematical nonsense if you are studying small numbers of people (e.g. 8 per cent of 23 children; 33 per cent of 6 children).

As a general rule, if you have:

- more than 100 subjects, then you can use statistical techniques;

- between 35 and 100 subjects, use percentages;

- between 12 and 35, you can use fractions, but beyond fifths use numbers (e.g. '6 of the children' not 'two-sevenths of the class');

- less than 12, use numbers (e.g. '3 out of the 7 children . . . '), but you can use 'half'.

Interpretive research

Interpretive research acknowledges that people actively construct a social world that is multi-layered, complex, in constant flux and state of change, evolving over time in response to participants' actions, understandings and reflections. As soon as someone enters a social situation they both influence it and are influenced by it, including a researcher.

Interpretive research:

- examines the natural setting (i.e. the researcher does not set up research tasks but observes what normally goes on);
- asks 'What is the meaning for *them?*' (rather than for *me*, the researcher);
- considers processes and/or relationships (how are they learning, rather than what have they learnt);
- acknowledges own beliefs, interests, experience and expertise, and accepts that findings are interpretations.

As you design your study, therefore, consider the factors that might influence the situation: will the children/the teachers/teaching assistants behave differently if you are watching? Try to minimise the impact of your presence. You should acknowledge such impacts as limitations on the validity of your study.

A key feature of the interpretive paradigm has been to 'make the familiar strange': an ability to step back from the experience of the everyday and consider what is noteworthy in the situation.

Example from practice

Emma had family in New York (NY). She was aware that routines of the Pre-school (NY) and the Reception class (UK) are so long established and familiar as to be taken for granted and 'How we do things' may actually have little rationale apart from custom. It was relatively easy to sit in the corner of the NY Pre-school and spot the differences in day-to-day practice. What she wanted to know was 'why?'. What might these differences tell her about the underlying ethos of education either side of the Atlantic? For instance, 'sharing' was more strongly promoted and reinforced in the NY setting ('How can we do this *together?*'), which she had also observed in parental intervention in playground disputes.

She identified themes across both settings that could be related to the norms of society, parental expectations, state/country government policy and the school curriculum that each setting was preparing the children to enter. It became a much more challenging project than she had imagined. She identified the main driver as 'What kind of citizens do we want these children to grow into?', which in turn made her reflect on her own practice and consider how the values she made explicit impacted on the classroom ethos and on the children's developing social selves. Looking deeply at a strangely familiar situation had enabled Emma to look again at her own practice differently.

Most interpretive studies employ qualitative data (Bruner's narrative ways of knowing) in order to illuminate a situation or establish personal perspectives and meaning-making. These methods are good for small-scale studies in which depth is preferred over breadth and for exploring areas of interest (but self-discipline is needed to avoid seeing what you want to see). The main area of difficulty is in making comparisons between studies of the same topic since there is no standardisation of approach or analysis.

Ethnography/grounded research

This is when the researcher goes into a situation with as few preconceptions as possible and by observation tries to work out what is going on. When this theory, or approach to research, arose, it was in conscious reaction to empiricist studies in which the researcher entered the setting with a hypothesis to test. It is closely allied to *participant observer research* in which the researcher becomes part of the community they are researching in order to understand the values and understandings of the culture they are researching.

It can easily be combined with other methods.

- An initial visit to observe the setting or having done a professional placement may provide ideas for your research question. Acknowledge this as part of your research.

- Asking just one open question might provide a large range of answers.

Case study

A case study is usually a small-scale study examining a single instance in detail, chosen to shed light on a particular problem or to answer a very specific question based on informal observations which have generated questions in the researcher's mind. Case studies are most frequently conducted qualitatively, using field notes, questioning, observation, audio or video recording. However, quantitative data might also be used to demonstrate the frequency of an observed behaviour.

Example from practice

Petr joined Matt's maths set speaking virtually no English, although it was soon apparent that his mathematical understanding was good. Matt felt that being placed in a lower maths set than his ability suggested meant that Petr was losing out on mathematical teaching that was more tailored to his existing knowledge. Although Petr was not the only child to join the school with very limited English, Matt had already built up a rapport with him as his maths teacher. A case study approach focusing on this one child was appropriate since Matt wanted to discover the child's viewpoint about his early days in the class so that, if someone else who didn't speak any English arrived, then Petr's experience might help Matt to support them more effectively.

Petr's answers gave Matt quite a surprise. He was quite happy in the low maths set. His ability to do the maths meant he could use these lessons to learn teacher talk and how to discuss ideas with his new friends which was useful in other lessons. Being confident with the maths gave him respect from his new friends as they quickly realised that he could help them with the maths if they helped him with the words. However, Petr became frustrated every time the special language teacher came along to remove him from the classroom, whatever lesson it was. He felt he was learning far more from real classroom interactions than from specific focused language teaching. He did not want to be picked out as not able to speak English; he was learning English as fast as he could anyway.

From conducting this case study, Matt obtained rich data that challenged his preconceptions. It was only because Matt asked for Petr's opinion that he was able to conceptualise him as a social agent within the learning environment.

We cannot generalise from this case study to say that all children are like Petr; we know they are not. Children are individuals; they are unpredictable; they are growing, living beings. But Matt's study reminds us that there is more to starting a new school in a new country than being placed in the right maths set. A case study can reveal insights that can be transferred and applied to other similar situations.

Action research

Action research is a cyclic research and development process, in which observations inform practice, leading to changes which are then further reflected upon and more changes made if needed.

Good action research should be:

- a testing ground for new ideas about pedagogy and practice;

- empowering teachers to be able to initiate change in the classroom;

- enabling teachers to challenge and ask deep, well-informed, open questions of themselves, of their situation, of underlying beliefs and assumptions.

Beware of assuming that your research is 'action research' just because you are doing it in a classroom and that action research is 'what teachers do'. Action research usually has an improvement goal in mind (e.g. 'How can I best help the children to gain mastery of a particular mathematical procedure?') and has a plan–do–reflect–change structure. You are *not* doing action research if your research is not reflexive and lacks a personal professional goal – i.e. if you are not analysing, reflecting on and changing *your own teaching*.

Example from practice

Michelle was interested in cue analysis. Did this enable children to better understand phonics? She was able to set up a longitudinal study and work with two groups of children. She introduced cue analysis to one group and after several weeks compared the progress of the two groups. Then the other group received the teaching and she intended to compare the results.

(Continued)

(Continued)

However, by the time she had completed the intervention, she had realised what the technique was good/less good for. This realisation informed her future teaching and was worth far more than the small difference in progress between the two groups of children. The outcome of her research had shifted from discovering whether or not a particular method of teaching phonics was effective, to a far deeper understanding of the *pedagogy* of phonics teaching. She now knew that cue analysis could be used effectively within the context of a whole suite of approaches, but more importantly, her research had enabled her to more deeply understand effective pedagogy in the teaching of phonics. This refection on practice, on her own teaching and the pedagogy that supported it, enabled her to be more confident and effective in her teaching. This is the primary aim of action research: to inform practice in such a way that the practitioner gains a deeper personal understanding of the underpinning pedagogy that will in turn significantly impact on their classroom practice.

Methodology goes viral: researching the Internet

Despite being accessible to so many people for so long, the use of the Internet as a source of research data within education is still low. Few texts on methodology deal with the issues at all, let alone adequately.

Reasons for using Internet data:

- You are researching public opinion (or the opinion of a specific section of the public).

- You want to compare your results with national trends.

- Your research shows that a particular teaching strategy works well/does not work as well as expected and you want to compare your sample with that of other researchers.

Say, for instance, a new teaching strategy has been introduced in your school and you want to find out if your observations, enthusiasm or misgivings are just personal, shared by others who have tried the same strategies, or even part of a national trend. One means of doing so would be to use web crawler software to trawl blogs relating to the topic. However, a fair amount of hands-on checking is required to ensure that blogs are not quoting blogs that are quoting blogs and that the whole thing goes round in a circle. You would also need to be aware that blogs are written by people with a particular commitment towards or against a topic so that the content is not unbiased.

What such a research technique might show, however, is how influential a particular blog/ feed or Twitter feed was by identifying those sites/feeds which receive the most links and hence are opinion formers. You could focus your search on links made within a particular week or month. Many people pass on a link to content they agree with or find helpful but you cannot assume this. The site with the most links might be the one that most people are reacting to and are passing on the link as a 'Have you read this??!!'.

More difficult to mine are social media such as Facebook and LinkedIn. However, if you have a group of peers whose opinions you want to research, then setting up a Facebook page might be a way forward. The problem is anonymity. Everyone who visits the page and leaves a comment is identifiable. However, you could build in a link to a blog or a page on your institution's VLE asking colleagues for help. For instance, you might ask them to:

- complete an online survey for you;

- try out and give feedback on an interactive resource you have created and hope to use in school;

- ask them to supply links to 'the most useful site for teaching . . . '.

Comments and links can then be left by your peers and you would then be able to analyse what they found useful.

Ethics

All research must be conducted in a manner that is moral, ethical and respectful to the research subjects. The methodology section of your essay or assignment needs an ethics section, even if you were required to submit an ethics form as part of the proposal. If this was written in considerable detail, it can be appropriate to refer to this in the main text in order to conserve word count (but make sure you include it in your appendices).

The following issues need to be considered.

- Trust: you are asking people to be open with you. Respect that. Act responsibly and take responsibility for the data you gather.

- Sensitivity: do not put in writing anything you could not say directly to someone's face. Imagine them reading it.

- Truth/validity: everything you conclude must be evidence based – never, ever, embroider the truth or recount half-remembered conversations.

- Unbiased fairness: we are all biased, we all have opinions but you must be dispassionate.

- Benefits: try to ensure there are benefits for the participants as well as yourself. Offer to share your research with the class teacher(s) or senior staff, or you may be able to immediately implement changes in your teaching that enhance children's learning.

- Personal matters: if you discover something confidential that might put you or someone else in a difficult situation, take advice from your research supervisor/ university tutor. If a child reveals something that you think might be a child protection issue, then speak to the member of staff responsible for this.

- If you conduct research abroad, especially in countries and/or contexts in which people are unaccustomed to research being undertaken in schools, they may blithely say 'Yes, yes, that's fine' without any apparent concern for the kind of ethical implications listed above. You yourself will then have to act as gatekeeper. What is fair, honest and respectful in this situation? In addition, you must ask yourself 'How well do I understand the social, cultural and political situation here?' before making any judgements about practice as you observe it.

For conducting research in the UK, you need to have a current Disclosure and Barring Service (DBS) certificate that covers you to work with children. You might also need this to cover you to work with vulnerable adults if, for instance, you were conducting research in a Special School in which some of the students were over 18. You do not need this, however, if your research is totally concerned with the knowledge or experiences of 'consenting' adults (i.e. those considered able to give their consent – e.g. teachers, parents, support staff) but you do need their consent to conduct the research. If you are conducting surveys or questionnaires among adults, then you can assume that if they complete and return it they are consenting to your use of their responses. You must, however, make this clear in a short paragraph at the top of the survey sheet.

Consent

You will need the consent of the management of the setting in which you will be working – usually referred to as the gatekeeper. However, you must not simply assume that if the headteacher or setting manager has agreed for you to conduct research that this provides blanket consent from everyone who works there. You will need consent from each teacher in whose class you wish to work and/or from each teaching assistant whose group of children you wish to observe while they are working with them. You will certainly need permission to peruse school or class data. If you wish to record (audio or video) the children you need to check this with the headteacher or gatekeeper – it might be that you cannot do so without formal written permission from parents so you might decide to take notes instead, or collect different kinds of data such as drawings which you can take away and look at later.

When conducting research with children, provided that the activity is one that they would normally do within their school day, you do not need specific permission from parents, although it would be polite to inform them via a class newsletter or a simple letter sent home with the children. However, formal, structured interviews with children are *not* part of the normal school day and require specific, written parental consent. If your research is a case study of one or a very few children, you must contact parents. If, however, you are examining how a sample group within a class benefit from a new teaching strategy you are at liberty to have a discussion with them to ascertain their viewpoint – it is part of what you might do anyway in the school context. This would be a form of semi-structured group interview (this is discussed further in the next chapter) and can be a valuable way to collect data in school contexts. You still need to ensure that all those participating understand that it is part of your research and that they have agreed to take part.

However, what happens if you try a new teaching method with one group of children and it is so successful that your group are now much better able to achieve a learning goal than other children? Obviously, the others should have the benefit of your new insight. But maybe the moment has passed; the class has moved on to another topic. Console yourself with the knowledge that this happens all the time in teaching. As you gain more experience and get better at the job and become more confident in trying new methods or ways of explaining things, all those previous classes have 'missed out' too. Simply acknowledge this ethical dilemma in your conclusions.

Assent

Whereas 'consent' is more formal, 'assent' is the less formal agreement to be part of what is going on at the time at which it occurs. You should make it clear to the children that although they cannot opt out of the lesson, they can choose for you not to include their work, their comment, their opinion and so on in the report you write about what you have discovered. Make it really clear to the children that you are not reporting on *them* but on what you are *learning about their learning*. Children usually respond well to becoming partners with you in the enterprise. I once had a child wait at least five minutes while I was providing practical help to a group and when she finally got my attention, she said 'Mrs Hope, I've just done something really interesting that I think you might want to write down in your book.' She had and I did!

Regardless of whether your research is with adults or children, they must be assured that all information they provide will be anonymous and securely stored and that access will be limited. You should not promise it will be destroyed for the following reasons.

- You will probably not delete every electronic copy.

- If you submit the assignment electronically (or use a checking device such as Turnitin), then you have no control over how long it is stored on your institution's hardware.

- If your assignment is published, then appendices showing children's work as well as your data analysis may enter the public domain.

The following broader issues can be thought about.

- Balance of power? You are 'teacher' or 'teacherly adult'. Do the children really believe they can opt out, especially if you give a questionnaire to the whole class? Can this really be classed as 'normal classroom practice'? Do they feel they need to give a 'right' answer rather than a truthful one?

- Ownership: who does your data belong to? The interpretation may be yours but the information belongs to the setting and the people there. Remember, children have rights too, which cannot be ignored just because they are little people in a situation in which they are expected to conform.

- Real anonymity? Could other insiders guess? How do you refer to people? Teacher X, Y etc., but what about the Special Educational Needs Co-Ordinator (SENCo) or the literacy co-ordinator? Children must be anonymised but it is difficult for the reader to follow Child A, B, C, D etc. You might find you get less confused as you write if you use real names in your first draft and then change the names afterwards.

Conclusion

The aim of this chapter has been to help you to understand what a methodology is and how to choose the right research strategy for answering your question(s). Duckworth (1987) in her well-named essay 'The Having of Wonderful Ideas' said:

> *Making new connections depends on knowing enough about something in the first place to provide a basis for thinking of other things to do – of other questions to ask – that demand more complex connections in order to make sense. The more ideas people already have at their disposal, the more new ideas occur and the more they can co-ordinate to hold up still more complicated structures.*

(Duckworth, 1987, p14)

To be able to make new connections and discover new ideas in your research journey, to see new things in the data, to be confident in your analysis, and to be able to make sense of your findings and to come to valid, insightful conclusions, you need to have chosen a well thought through methodology. Hopefully, this chapter has enabled you to begin to do that.

Things to think about

1. Have you written a research question in such a way that it is clear what kind of data you will need to collect?

2. Which data will best answer your question: numbers or words or both?

3. What are the ethical issues which are specific to your context?

4. What are your biases – your personal investment in the area you are investigating?

5. What methodological literature will you need to reference in your methodology write-up?

References

Bruner, J (1986) *Actual Minds, Possible Worlds*. New York: Harvard University Press.

Duckworth, E (1987) *The Having of Wonderful Ideas*. New York: Teachers College Press.

Hope, G (2003) A holistic view of assessing young children's designing. In Benson, C and Till, W, *Conference Proceedings: The Third International Primary Design and Technology Conference (CRIPT)*. Birmingham, Birmingham City University, June.

Middleton, H (2000) Design and technology: What is the problem? In Kimbell, R (ed.) *Design and Technology International Millennium Conference*. Wellesbourne, Warwickshire: The Design and Technology Association.

Rittel, H and Webber, MM (1969) *Wicked Problem*. In Cross, N, Elliott, D and Roy, R, *Man-Made Futures*. Milton Keynes: Open University Press.

Further reading

Arthur, J, Waring, M, Coe, R and Hedges, LV (2013) *Research Methods and Methodologies in Education*. London: SAGE.

Clough, P and Nutbrown, C (2002) *A Student's Guide to Methodology: Justifying Research*. London: SAGE.

Cohen, L, Manion, L and Morrison, C (2007) *Research Methods in Education*. London: Routledge.

McNiff, J (2010) *Action Research for Professional Development: Concise Advice for New and Experienced Researchers*. Dorset: September Books.

Punch, KF and Oancea, A (2014) *Introduction to Research Methods in Education*. London: SAGE.

Taylor, C, Wilkie, M and Baser, J (2006) *Doing Action Research*. London: SAGE.

Ethics

Follow the guidance offered by the British Education Research Association (BERA) available at: www.bera.ac.uk

Chapter 6

Research methods: how will I collect the data?

Wendy Cobb

Objectives

This chapter:

- examines the purpose, strengths and limitations of different data collection methods;
- discusses the practicalities involved when implementing different approaches to data collection.

Chapter summary

How you will collect the data you need requires careful consideration of the strengths and weaknesses of a range of research methods so that you can select and justify your approach.

Introduction

By this stage you should have a fairly good idea of your research question and who your participants will be. The previous chapter has helped you consider some of the bigger questions in relation to how to go about collecting the information you need in order to investigate the answers to your question. This chapter will explore in more depth the practical considerations you might need to address when employing some of the more common approaches to data collection in research in primary schools. The chapter is divided into two sections: the first section focuses on interviews and questionnaires; the second section focuses on data collected through observations and artefacts such as children's drawings, photographs or created objects.

Interviews and questionnaires

One of the easiest and most straightforward ways to find out what you want to know is to ask your participants questions. You can do this orally in the form of a face-to-face interview or you can get answers to your questions in written form through a questionnaire. The approach you use will depend on factors such as; the nature of the data you want to collect; the number of participants you are working with; who your participants are; your relationship with the participants; and the time you have available.

Asking questions might seem like an easy data-gathering option. However, flick between the many television channels currently available and you may notice some differences in technique between experienced and inexperienced interviewers and how a poorly chosen question can quickly close down an interview. You yourself might also have given up half-way through a questionnaire because you were put off by the way the questions were asked or what they were asking. Successful research interviews and questionnaires require careful thought and planning so that you can be confident they will do the job you need them to.

Interviews and questionnaires, while they both ask direct questions of the participants, are used to elicit very different types of data. Interviews are generally more personal and interactive, and you are more able to develop an understanding of people's experiences, feelings and perceptions about things. They can be undertaken with individuals or with groups. They are good if the question you are asking looks to find out 'why' rather than 'what'. Interviews are very challenging if you have large numbers of participants because they are generally time-consuming and require high levels of engagement from both interviewer and participants. As discussed in the last chapter, you will also need to consider ethical issues – formal, structured interviews with children will require explicit written consent from their parents.

Questionnaires tend to be more detached and formal, and are good for finding out discrete 'facts' such as 'how often . . . ?'; 'what do you eat/read/do when . . . ?'; 'how many . . . ?' and so on. They are also useful if you are looking for quantifiable data about responses. For example, you can have sliding scales which allow the participant to indicate degrees of response – for example, from 'very interested' to 'not at all interested'. They are a useful way to get information from a large number of participants, especially if you are able to schedule a time for your participants to complete the questionnaire – for example, as part of lesson time.

The kind of data you get from questionnaires can often be represented in numerical form in tables and graphs whereas data from interviews is more likely to generate narrative data (data that 'tells a story' – as described in the previous chapter) and the researcher looks for themes or similarities and differences in the responses. Chapter 7 looks at the analysis of the different types of data in more detail, but it is worth thinking about it here, too, as part of the planning process. In the debates around research in education the kind of data generated through questionnaires is sometimes argued for as more objective and more 'accurate' because the interviewer is detached from the responses given by the participants. The data generated can be 'number crunched' and where large numbers of participants have been surveyed, this can provide seemingly objective statistical data which can be used in developing policy and practice. In Chapter 5 Gill Hope explained this more fully and in Chapter 2 Judy Durrant discussed the very large-scale, randomised controlled trials which are often referred to in government policy documents and some of the issues surrounding these in terms of primary education. There is a strong argument, though, that interviews, despite the potential influence and bias from the interviewer, provide richer data which better represents the complexities of lived experience in the social world – the 'fuzziness' that Gill Hope referred to. If you use interviews you are less likely, perhaps, to be thinking about finding a generalisable 'truth' but rather exploring responses which are more personal and context-bound. Whatever approach you take, in your methodology section of your research report you will need to acknowledge the strengths and weaknesses of your chosen method. There is not a 'right' or 'wrong' way to collect data – you just need to be able to justify why you have chosen the tool you have. This chapter, along with the previous one, will help you to formulate those arguments.

Example from practice

A large primary school has recently introduced a new type of homework club and has received funding for a six-week pilot. Although all children in Year 6 were eligible to apply to join the club, invitations were targeted at vulnerable groups. Fifteen children, from four classes have attended the pilot. The Senior Management Team (SMT) needs evidence of the impact of the pilot in order to decide whether to allocate funding to continue and extend the initiative. Maria, a Year 6 teacher who is also a Master's student with an interest in pupil, parent and staff voice, offers to survey staff, parent and child perceptions of the benefit of the clubs on pupil learning for her next research assignment.

After reading some research literature for initial guidance, Maria discusses the strengths and weaknesses of different research approaches with her Master's group colleagues and the deputy head teacher at her school.

Below are the research methods Maria discusses. Each of these methods will give her a different kind of data and therefore provide different information about her research focus.

- Parent questionnaire.
- Staff questionnaire.
- Telephone interview with parents.
- Staff group interviews.
- Staff individual interviews.
- Group interview with Year 6 pupils.

In her initial research proposal Maria rejects the idea of using a written questionnaire for parents and opts for structured telephone interviews. However, she decides to develop a short questionnaire to help select a sample of staff for a small number of semi-structured interviews. She plans to pilot her interview questions within her Master's group and gather some more advice on interviewing techniques before carrying out the staff and parent interviews. Maria also decides to set up a pupil focus group to take place during assembly time and discuss how to manage the group and observation recordings with the TA. She is aware that she will need to gain consent/assent from all respondents participating in the research.

Interviews

In small-scale classroom-based investigations it is likely that interviews will be a useful way to collect data. In the context of a small-scale project a well-constructed, thirty-minute long semi-structured group interview with just a few children can generate plenty of data for a research report. Collecting too much data is a common mistake made by novice researchers. Far better to have a small amount of high quality data which can be examined in depth than a mass of data which ends up being reported or described rather than analysed when it comes to the writing up. The next chapter revisits this and suggests how you might deal with too much (or too little) data.

If you decide to use interviews, you need to consider the kind of interview which best meets your research needs and your own level of research skill. As mentioned earlier, interviews are not as easy as you might think. You need to consider whether you will interview individuals or groups, where you will interview them, your relationship with the interviewees and how you interact with them, how you put them at their ease and how you respond to their reactions through the interview. And, of course, you will need to decide how to formulate questions which will elicit the required responses. All of these factors will influence the data that you get from your participants.

The influence of the researcher

As mentioned above, one of the criticisms of interviews is that the interviewer necessarily has an influence on the outcomes. In large-scale projects this is sometimes overcome by having people other than the researcher undertaking the interviews using a standard set of questions without any further follow-up or probing of the answers. These kinds of interviews are called structured interviews and are really more like a spoken form of questionnaire. You are unlikely to be in a position to be able to use research assistants in this way, although it is increasingly common to find researchers asking children to interview their peers to gain a different perspective.

An alternative is to acknowledge, up front, that if you, the researcher, are undertaking the interviews then you are going to affect the data that you collect. This is not necessarily a negative point but you need to be aware of it, be open about it in your writing up and consider it carefully in the analysis of your data.

Think about the following.

- How well do you know the participants?

- Are you their teacher? Their colleague? A visitor?

- Is there any reason why the participants might not feel able to be completely open in their responses to you?

- Is there anything about you that your participants might find intimidating or threatening?

- What is the nature of the power imbalance between you and your interviewees?

While you need to consider each of these factors before, during and after interviews, when you write up your research you are acknowledging the context in which you collected the data. However, you don't need to apologise for it – there just isn't the perfect scenario.

Undertaking interviews with children you know well because you have taught them for a sustained period of time might well mean that they are more relaxed and open with you, and you have better insights into the children beyond the interview context. On the other hand, it might mean that they are simply keen to please you as their teacher. If you interview children whom you have never met, you might find that there is an awkwardness to your conversations as you do not know each other, but they might be more open to giving you replies which are critical and reflective.

There are always power issues in any research context. Where you are interviewing children these issues will need to be acknowledged and/or mitigated against. You might want to play down your 'teacher' role by dressing casually and introducing yourself by your first name or you might simply maintain the role that the children are used to you being in and interpret their responses accordingly. Sometimes the power issues might relate to participants' perceptions that you are being critical or judging them through your research – if you are researching practice in your own school context you will need to be sensitive to the ways in which you conduct your research. If, for example, you are considering how questioning is used in the classroom and you are observing and/or talking to teaching assistants, teachers and the head teacher, you will need to be sure that your questions are sensitive and do not imply fault. For example, you wouldn't ask: 'Why don't you use more open questions?' Researching practice in any setting needs to be tackled sympathetically (whatever your method of data collection) and the purpose and outcomes of the research need to be clear to all involved.

Individual or group?
There are a number of good reasons for interviewing both adults and children in groups. It is clearly less intimidating for them and the interaction between members of

the group can add to the detail and complexity of responses. The same question might stimulate five minutes of conversation in a group yet elicit only a short, one-sentence reply in a one-to-one context.

Consider the following.

> The group interview has the advantages of being inexpensive, data rich, flexible, stimulating to respondents, recall aiding, and cumulative and elaborative, over and above individual responses.

(Denzin and Lincoln, 1998, p55)

The downside of this statement is that the members of the group will interact with each other and might affect their responses, meaning that you don't always uncover the perspectives of each individual member.

> The emerging group culture may interfere with individual expression, the group may be dominated by one person, the group format makes it difficult to research sensitive topics . . . the requirements for interviewer skills are greater because of group dynamics.

(Ibid., p55)

When designing your own research project you need to choose an approach that will give you the best answers to your question.

Designing the approach to the interview

Interviews, be they group or individual, can take various forms for research purposes. You are trying to get answers to questions and you will need to have an idea about how you will get at the information you need from your participants. As we said earlier, it is not as easy as it looks.

Types of interview to consider are as follows.

- **Structured interview** The researcher uses the same set of questions prepared in advance and which may have a limited range of possible answers. It is more like a questionnaire than an interview – the researcher does not probe the interviewee or attempt to go beyond the set questions. It can be a useful approach to take if the participants might have some difficulty with writing responses in a questionnaire but you want to use questionnaire-style questions. You need to carefully plan your questions, but undertaking the interview itself requires minimal interviewer skill.

- **Semi-structured interview** This is a good approach for new researchers. You might prepare in advance a set of questions or topic areas which you are going to explore, but you pursue the interviewees' answers so that you are able to follow through interesting ideas or themes which arise. If you are undertaking semi-structured interviews with more than one group of participants you might find that you cover quite different ground with different groups as you follow different threads of the conversation. This needs to be acknowledged when analysing and reporting on your data.

- **Unstructured interview** This approach requires a very high skill level. You will need a clear idea of the areas to be covered in the interview, linked to the research question and you should have some notes to guide the interview. However, the interview itself is unstructured. Questions tend to be open-ended. If you take this approach you can listen sensitively to what the participants are saying and adjust your questions to suit. King and Horrocks (2010, p35) argue that you 'must be able to respond to the issues that arise during the interview' and that a flexible interview guide 'allows the participant to lead the interaction in unanticipated directions'.

- **Informal conversations** These should be used with great caution. You can only make use of incidental conversations or discussions with participants if they form part of your research design. You must ensure that the participants have agreed to this in advance in accordance with ethical procedures and that they are aware that the conversation might be used in your research. Data gathered in this way might emerge through conversations with participants in the field – for instance, at break times in the staffroom or at the end of the day. You might carry a jotter to collect field notes or try to remember the conversation to record at a later time.

Asking questions

Whether you select open/closed questions or direct/indirect questions or a combination of these will depend on the type of information you are seeking to find out from your research question and who you are interviewing. You are more likely to use closed questions with very young children and to select polite, indirect questions (such as 'could you tell me . . . ?', 'I was wondering if . . . ?) when you are interviewing people you don't know very well or when you want to put people at ease.

Patton (1990, cited in King and Horrocks, 2010, p36) argues that there are six types of questions that can be used in qualitative interviews, although there are some crossovers between categories.

- You might use closed 'background/demographic questions' to find out personal characteristics of the participants such as name, age, gender, etc.

- 'Experience/behaviour questions' can be used to explore specific actions that took place ('What happened when . . . ?).

- 'Opinion/values questions'. For instance, Maria might ask staff 'What did you hope to achieve by piloting the homework club?'.

- King and Horrocks (2010, p36) suggest that 'feelings questions' must be worded in a way that makes clear to the participant that you want to explore emotional responses. For instance, 'What feelings did that provoke in you?' would be more effective than 'How did you feel about it?'. The former question acknowledges that a range of feelings can be elicited from a single experience.

- 'Knowledge questions' seek to elicit facts rather than opinions. For instance, Maria might ask, 'What did you know about the homework club before you decided to pilot it?'. Consider the different response this question might elicit compared to the question, 'What was your opinion of the homework club before piloting it?'. Of course, there is no guarantee that the first question will elicit a more factual response than the second question, however, Cohen et al. (2013, p417) argue that 'inaccuracy and bias may be minimized by careful structuring of the questions'.

- 'Sensory questions' elicit information about sensory aspects of experience. You might ask the participant what they saw, heard, touched, tasted or smelled in the situation.

We will consider some particular pitfalls that can arise in the choice of questions when we explore questionnaires in more detail.

Conducting the interview

First, you will need to decide where the interview should take place. Choose a setting with few distractions such as bright lights and loud noises, where you are unlikely to be interrupted (we mentioned before that Sackes et al. (2010)) chose to interview their participants individually in a quiet room with few distractions. If you are conducting one-to-one interviews with staff you might be able to arrange to do this off site. If you are conducting a group interview with children choose a location that they will be familiar with and comfortable in. This might be a classroom during assembly time. You might need to book a room and/or put a 'do not disturb' note on the library. Consider also the layout of the furniture – what chairs will you use and how will you position them? Check that the interviewee is comfortable and help them to feel comfortable by engaging in some 'small talk' before beginning the formal interview. This is easier if you know something about your interviewees, so plan ahead. If you can build a rapport early on the interviewees are more likely to relax and regard you as a trustworthy interviewer.

You will also need to think about how to begin the interview. Denscombe (2010) suggests that establishing trust and rapport is crucial to the successful interview. Begin by explaining the purpose and format of the interview. Address the issue of confidentiality. Explain who will have access to the responses and how you will analyse the answers. Adhere to the school safeguarding policy by not promising that you can keep everything confidential. Explain how you will record quotes and get permission from the respondents for this. If you have a colleague in the room to record responses or write observational notes, introduce them and explain their role. Denscombe adds that you should start with an easy question, such as a background question, which will 'offer the chance for the interviewee to settle down and relax' (p185). You will also need to ensure that all the ethical procedures have been completed – assent might need to be ascertained at the beginning of the interview if this has not been done before.

When you are interviewing there are a number of techniques you can use to make your interviews as effective as possible. You can use verbal and visual cues such as open body language which is welcoming and comforting. Nodding, maintaining eye contact and using gesture or verbal responses ('yes', 'I see') to acknowledge understanding will demonstrate that you are engaged and listening to the responses.

You can paraphrase your participants' responses, although effective paraphrasing is not as simple as it seems. McNiff and Whitehead (2010, p164) suggest you use a phrase such as 'Now, as I understand it, you are saying . . . '. However, you need to be careful not to lead the interviewee to agree with your interpretation of the question response. You may need to draw the interviewee back to the research question by restating your initial question in the paraphrase. You can also check that you have paraphrased accurately by asking 'Are you happy that I understand you?'/'Have I said that correctly?'. You might also ask the interviewee to put a question in their own words to check their understanding.

You will need to demonstrate sensitivity to interviewee responses to questions; if you sense a question may be uncomfortable or controversial ask/check that the respondent is happy to discuss the subject: 'Is it OK to talk about this?'.

Silence is not always a bad thing in interviews. McNiff and Whitehead (ibid.) consider silences as 'important spaces in which people gather their thoughts or harness their courage' so you should 'accept silences and be silent yourself' (p164).

If your interviewee is happy for you to record the interview, you will want any recording to be as unobtrusive as possible. You could choose to write field notes, either during the interview or immediately afterwards. Field notes enable you to add contextual information more easily than if you choose to use an audio or visual recording. However, the interviewee may disagree with your interpretation of the interview and you will need to acknowledge any potential for misinterpretation and bias in your write-up. You can partially address this by asking the interviewee to check the transcribed notes, although this might not be practicable. You will find information about transcription methods in the analysis chapter.

As mentioned in the previous chapter, it is essential that you have sought and gained permission if you are audio- or video-recording the interview.

Elicitation techniques

Sometimes the nature of your research question means that questioning your participants might not quite get at what it is you want to know. If you are trying to uncover something about unconscious behaviours or thought processes, then direct questions might be very difficult for your participants to answer and you might need to approach the subject in a more roundabout way.

In these cases it is often very useful to combine a semi-structured group interview with some form of elicitation technique. This is an activity or focus for the interview which is used to elicit participants' responses in a less direct way. For example, children might draw a picture of a 'princess' as part of a research project which asks about children's understanding of the princess archetype in traditional tales. The children participate in a semi-structured, small group interview while they do their drawings and the drawings are used both as a means by which talk is generated (the interviewer can ask questions about the drawing), and as data in their own right.

The second section of this chapter includes examples of elicitation techniques and the data beyond the interview – that is, the drawings, models, photographs and other artefacts that you might ask participants to produce – but the use of an elicitation device within the interview context is worth considering.

Questionnaires

There is an episode of *Yes Minister* where Humphrey, the Minister's adviser, explains to Bernard, the Minister's secretary, how two differently worded questionnaires could lead to opposite answers to the question 'Should we bring back conscription?'. It is very easy – even unconsciously – to skew the results in a particular way. Questionnaires are not straightforward. Bell (2010, p140) describes questionnaires as being *'fiendishly difficult* "to design, requiring" *discipline in the selection of questions, in question writing, in the design, piloting, distribution and return of the questionnaires'*. McNiff and Whitehead (2010) urge caution to the first-time researcher and highlight the influences that questionnaires can have on the respondents.

Precise wording is important in the questionnaire design. Let's imagine Maria considers asking parents, 'Has participating in the homework club had a positive impact on your child's attitude towards school work?' and suggests providing a set of possible responses such as 'A lot', 'Quite a bit', 'A little' or 'Not at all'. How will she interpret the results? Parents may interpret the phrase 'positive impact' in different ways and may have different perceptions of what constitutes 'A lot' or 'A little'. This question might need to become four or five separate questions which are more specific about 'positive impact'.

As Bell (2010) suggests, respondents may leave items blank or abandon questionnaires if they are confused or irritated by the question. A parent might think that the question in the paragraph above assumes that their child had a negative attitude towards school before joining the homework club, and might also assume that the school believes it is the parent's fault. A better question might be, 'Has your child's attitude towards schoolwork changed since joining the club?' or 'Does your child show less interest in schoolwork/the same interest in schoolwork/ more interest in school work?'.

Assumptions can also lead to false memories. Perhaps the above question has now planted a false memory of the parent's child having a poor attitude towards school before joining the club. This might impact on the parent's memory of how much the child enjoyed school previously.

fictional example from practice is just one example of a situation where a
y designed questionnaire *might* be appropriate. If Maria does decide that a
questionnaire is an appropriate data collection method for her study, she will have
one chance to get the design right to encourage as many staff to complete the survey
as fully as possible. Denscombe (2010, p162) advises keeping questionnaires as brief
as possible '*by reducing the scope of the questions to crucial issues related to the research and
avoiding any superfluous detail or non-essential topics'.*

In addition to considering potential issues with the wording of the questionnaire
mentioned previously, you could also consider the following questions.

Are all the questions vital to the research?	If you are asking about homework, don't ask questions about the child's responses to work in school. What are the absolutely key issues which you want to find out about?
Are there any duplicate questions which ask the same thing in different ways? Are they necessary?	There is no need to ask respondents to list both their age and their date of birth. However, duplicate questions can be justified as a form of triangulation. Asking 'Does your child ask for help with their homework?' as well as 'Does your child find homework difficult?' can give you a more nuanced set of responses.
Is the task of responding to the survey easy and quick?	Test how long it takes to complete the questionnaire and adjust if too long. If you are using electronic media, is the system easily navigable and glitch free?

Using questionnaires with children

If you are considering using questionnaires with children you will want to ensure
that the experience is positive for each child. Questionnaires can be designed that
are appealing – for instance, by careful choice of font and the inclusion of pictures.
Questions need to be age appropriate and relevant. Careful choice needs to be taken
about the use of vocabulary and how the survey will be administered. Self-completion
surveys can be administered using a paper and pencil or a child might complete
answers directly into a laptop. Consider, though, how challenging reading questions
might be for children with a young reading age or with disabilities. A teacher or
teaching assistant could read the questions for the child, or audio recording technology
could be used. For instance, a child could listen to the questions through headphones
and answer on the computer, replaying the questions several times.

Bell (2007, p463) recognises that children may be affected by the content and context
of questions and other aspects of the survey, such as the physical setting, in a different
way to adults. However, she believes that survey research with children is feasible from
around the age of seven, with carefully adapted questionnaires, and considers some
questionnaire design 'dos and don'ts'. Your child questionnaire dos and don'ts need to
be context specific, but here are some general points you should consider.

- Is the language simple, unambiguous, age-appropriate and relevant?

- Is the layout appealing?

- Have you used positive questions wherever possible?

- Do the questions demand too high a level of memory recall?

- Have you provided a limited number of options?

- Could you use visual labels (e.g. smiley faces) on scales rather than numeric labels (which can be more challenging for children)?

Example from practice

Bakx et al. (2015) conducted a study into pupils' perceptions of teacher quality in primary education. As most of the studies they reviewed involved older children's perceptions, they wanted to develop a suitable way to assess and explore primary pupils' views. A total of 2,514 pupils aged between 5 and 12 completed an open-ended questionnaire anonymously as part of a lesson activity in a number of schools. The researchers created a question-naire which they called the 'teacher-spider' because it looked like a spider. It contained one open-ended question: 'What is a good teacher?' In their research report they explain that, although similar to a mind map, the teacher-spider contains no hierarchy or layers. As top-ics do not need to be presented in a hierarchal order, the authors argue that it is easier for young pupils to create a teacher-spider.

The following is a summary of some key considerations when you create questionnaires.

- What is the purpose of the survey?

- How do the questions relate to the aims of the research?

- What is your sample group? (Who is likely to have the information you need?)

- Will you use open or closed questions or a mixture of both?

- Are any questions biased or misleading?

- Can the respondents be expected to read and understand the questions?

- Are all the questions crucial to the research?

- Is the layout of the questionnaire clear and logical?

- Is the questionnaire brief and manageable? (Have you piloted the survey?)

- How will the questionnaire be administered?

- How will you record and analyse the results?

- What permissions will you need to seek?

Observations and artefacts

This second section of the chapter will review some approaches to gathering different kinds of data. If interviews or questionnaires might be limiting in what they can tell you, you might like to consider observations which tell you about the actions and activities of your participants, or the use of artefacts which might provide you with more a tangential insight into your participants' thinking and/or provide a more tangible way for your participants, to express themselves. I have also included in this section some approaches to collecting rich data through less familiar elicitation techniques to give you an idea of the range of techniques available to you as a researcher.

Observation

If you are an Early Years practitioner you are likely to be confident already in the use of observation as a technique for gathering pupil progress data. Observational research throughout the primary years can benefit from the observational practices of the Early Years classroom. Your task as a researcher is to be systematic in both your data recording and data analysis, and to go beyond merely looking and listening. If you have no Early Years experience, you are still a veteran observer. From a tiny baby you will have been using your senses to gather and select information about the world around you. However, you will need to refine your skills to become a systematic and effective observational researcher.

> *Observation offers the social researcher a distinct way of collecting data. It does not rely on what people say they do, or what they say they think. It is more direct than that. Instead, it draws on the direct evidence of the eye to witness events at first hand. It is based on the premise that, for certain purposes, it is best to observe what actually happens.*

(Denscombe, 2010, p196)

The following are some of the advantages of observation.

- You can observe behaviour as it is happening.

- You are not relying on potentially misleading reported accounts (consider the list of issues we explored with the language of interviews and questionnaires).

- There is a large degree of flexibility in the choice of observational method and you can be responsive to the situation.

- You can collect a permanent record of an event.

- You can triangulate the data with data collected through other research methods.

The following are some of the disadvantages of observation.

- Observation can be time-consuming and resource intensive.

- Observer bias: the observation record might be inaccurate or one-sided; no matter how hard you try to be objective, you may only see what you expect to see.

- Observer effect: your presence as observer may influence those being observed so that you do not see usual behaviour.

Systematic enquiry requires a degree of selection and focus, but there are a vast array of options available to you in your choice of observational method from a very structured approach (likely to come from a positivist perspective and linked to quantifiable data) to a more flexible unstructured approach. A very structured approach to observation in the primary years is likely to include some or all of the following aspects.

Aspect	Example
A clear purpose linked tightly to the research question	Question: How effectively do children make use of the available classroom resources? Purpose of observation: to find out if pupils use available resources in the classroom and whether they do so independently or under the direction of staff.
A clear focus for the observation	To survey one group of six children's use of classroom resources.
A planned setting	Year 3 classroom.
A time frame	Observations will take place in three lessons across one day.
A planned recording method	The observer will record against a list of the children's names the resources each child uses in each lesson. A coding system will be used to identify independent and teacher/TA directed used of resources.
A data analysis method	The data will be analysed to identify the most common resources used independently/under the teacher's direction. Children's results will be compared to see if there is consistency across the group.

Another structured method that the observer could use linked to the above purpose is to map out on a classroom plan the movement of the children around the room. The observer would then be able to analyse which resource areas are used most in each lesson.

These two examples of interactive coding systems enable the observer to make an objective record with no need for observer judgement and so avoid the risk of observer bias through the recording. Of course, there is a risk of observer effect as the children may change their behaviour if they know they are being observed and know the purpose of the observation.

If your research includes a study of classroom dynamics, playground interactions or the changing perceptions of a peer group over a period of time, then you will be engaging in ethnography, which is the study of behaviours, interactions and perceptions of people and groups in different settings. In ethnographic research the observer often becomes immersed in the setting as participant observer collecting detailed field notes. In the first example from practice, below, the researcher explains that she has taken an ethnographic approach to her research but makes a case for her position as non-participant observer. In the second example from practice the researchers have adopted an opposite position as participant observers and provide a different rationale for their choice of approach.

Example from practice

Jarvis (2010, p65) carried out research investigating young children's rough-and-tumble (R&T) play. Her study was framed around three research questions.

- 'What narratives can be found within R&T, and how can we use these to understand what the play means to children?
- Do the narratives that children use in R&T differ with respect to gender?
- What might such narratives tell us about complex social learning and skill development taking place within R&T?'

Jarvis's research took place over an 18-month period in a medium-sized primary school. The sample group (18 children) comprised the eldest nine children of each gender in their year group. This is how Jarvis explains her choice of method.

> The research focused on their outdoor free play from their final term in nursery and into their first term in Year 1 (aged 4.5–6 years). The research used non-participant observation in which I endeavoured to ensure that the children would act as naturally as possible during observations. For example, I spent time with them, modelling my role on that of a parent-helper who did not engage in any type of interaction relating to behaviour issues. I spent time talking to the children about their play (including asking for their permission to observe, which was also formally requested from their parents in writing). During their last term in nursery, the children became used to me walking around their outdoor play area, speaking quietly into a dictaphone. This method was chosen because more data could be gathered in real time in speech than by note-taking, and it was not as intrusive or technologically demanding as videotaping. The principal technique used for the observations was that of 'focal child' when each participant was observed for one hour in total, across different play periods.

> (Jarvis, 2010, pp.65–6)

From this short extract Jarvis has already explained a number of steps she has taken to justify the validity of her chosen research method. She has:

- used a system for selecting her sample group by focusing on the eldest nine children in each year group;
- attempted to limit the observer effect by modelling her role on that of a parent-helper and not engaging in any type of interaction relating to behaviour issues;
- focused her observations on play;

- spoken quietly into a dictaphone which enables immediate recording and limits the intrusiveness of the recording method;

- used the same approach over an 18-month period;

- focused on one child at a time;

- allocated the same amount of observation time to each child.

Below is an example of how Jarvis records her observations.

> Boys' game: James is play-punching Andy with sound effects ('pow, pow'), Andy is chopping at James. Later they tell me that the chopping motion is Mr Psycho's hammer.

> Girls' game: Vicky has her hands up by the side of her head (rabbit ears). She runs away and then back to Emily. Emily puts her hands around Vicky and then Marina comes and puts her arms around them both . . . the game also seems to involve Vicky and Marina getting just so close that Emily can nearly touch them, then they laugh and pull back.

> (Jarvis, 2010, p67)

Jarvis transcribes her recording as spoken in real time in the present tense. She records what she can see and acknowledges when she is making a comment based on her perception 'the game also seems to involve . . . '

Participant observation

Example from practice

Coates and Coates (2006) carried out research over a three-year period into young children talking and drawing in nursery and reception settings. They identified two over-arching aims for their research, which were to:

> explore the relationship between young children's drawing and any accompanying narrative; consider the implications of this relationship for our understanding of children's creative and conceptual development.

> (Coates and Coates, 2006, p225)

In contrast to Jarvis's (2010) choice of a non-participatory approach to observational research, Coates and Coates decided to act as participant observers. The following is how they explain their choice of approach.

> the [children] were supplied with drawing media and asked to make images of subjects of their own choice. The researchers' role was to immerse themselves in the context in which the drawings were being made, not as detached observers, but as participant observers, playing an active part in the children's conversations and acting as a focus for their questions and insights when the need arose . . . Success in eliciting self-directed drawings and encouraging related narratives depended almost entirely on the researchers' ability

> (Continued)

(Continued)

> to establish empathic and harmonious relationships in a non-threatening context, based on mutual trust and a familiarity of the situations in which the children worked . . . Skills both as teachers of and communicators with young children proved useful in establishing appropriate relationships. The researchers' utterances, rather than directive, aimed by means of prompting, encouraging and social talk to persuade children to extend their visual explorations and spoken discourse, and enhance their confidence in the worth of these by the means of approval and positive reinforcement. The results of each episode, therefore, were entirely unique, deeply personal and incapable of replication.
>
> (Coates and Coates, 2006, p226)

Coates and Coates explain how they are attempting to avoid the observer effect by immersing themselves into the children's worlds and developing empathic, harmonious and trusting relationships. Rather than directing the children's perceptions, they are aiming to encourage open dialogue and support the development of the children's confidence in spoken dialogue and visual explorations. Their intention is for the children to have a positive outcome from participation in the research.

The following are some of the advantages of participant observation.

- It could be argued that immersing yourself as a participant in the setting is the only way of properly understanding the culture of the context.

- It allows more scope for you to uncover factors that you could not have predicted at the start of the research as you are more in tune with the context.

The following are some of the disadvantages of participant observation.

- It is very time-consuming (participant observation is generally more relevant for longitudinal research).

- As you are part of the research you inevitably affect the outcomes.

- It is difficult to record data when you are actively participating.

- It is subjective – it is very hard to remain objective when you are part of the research so there is a real danger of personal bias.

Elicitation techniques

If you choose to use an observation method for your research you could decide to combine your observation with another elicitation method as in the above research study. As mentioned before, you could also choose to combine a form of interview, such as a focus group, with an elicitation technique. Barton (2015, p180) suggests that elicitation techniques can *facilitate such conversations by displacing the focus of interviews onto external stimuli and, in some cases, changing the power balance between researchers and participants*. He also argues that *familiarity with a range of such techniques can help researchers collect rich data even on difficult topics*.

Some of the more common types of elicitation techniques include the use of mind maps, musical stimuli and photo-elicitation (the use of photos, videos and other forms of visual representation). When I was studying for my Master's degree, I engaged in a research workshop where we explored the use of collage to express perceptions of our current reality. I became fully immersed in the activity, ripping pages from magazines and frenziedly sticking and layering images. I photographed my created collage, wrote field notes in my journal about the experience to help explore my understanding of myself as a teacher-leader and subsequently included an annotated picture of the collage as part of the supporting data for my final Master's dissertation.

Example from practice

Austin (2014) undertook research which looked at children's identity in transition from primary to secondary school. She needed a means by which she could find out about what the children thought about who they were and how others saw them. Below is an explanation of the approach she took with small groups of Year 6 children.

As an adult who was previously unknown to them I felt that these Phase One interviews would be best undertaken with groups. This offered a more relaxed atmosphere as the children knew and were comfortable with each other and could interact with each other as well as with me. In addition I wanted to avoid the uncomfortable, unnatural turn taking responses that might arise from a group discussion, such as when formally sitting in a semi-circle or round a table. The children were therefore given the task of drawing a picture of how they imagined they might be when they were in Year 7. This was set as the 'purpose' of the interview but acted also as a means of facilitating more natural conversation around the key research questions. The drawings themselves constituted a further representation (along with what they said) of their identity performance both for the present and the projected future. The use of drawing in this way was supportive of a loosely structured interview approach.

Some elements of the key questions for the research were asked directly, for example: "What do you think you will be like when you are in Year 7?" (A question also addressed through the drawing activity). However other data were gathered through the ways in which the children talked about themselves, about each other (and other peers), to each other and to me. The interviews were therefore reflexively constitutive of data which could, in the one event of the interview context, offer potential for drawing together aspects of what might count as identity work from three different perspectives: their talk about self, their talk about others and their drawings.

(Austin, 2014, pp56–7)

Austin also describes how the use of drawings meant that silences in the interview were more easily tolerated. In addition, she explains how the drawings themselves naturally elicited questions from the researcher and the other children in the group, enriching the data further and allowing it to be child-centred. She acknowledges, too, that drawings as a source of data have some limitations.

(Continued)

(Continued)

I explained to the children that they could also add words or writing to their pictures if they would like to and I offered children the opportunity to write if they were unsure how they could put something they wanted to communicate in a drawing. The strength of this approach was that it provided an extra dimension to the data collected – and enabled some further clarification of the thinking with which the children were engaging. However it is acknowledged that whilst for some children drawings were an accessible and enjoyable way to communicate through the research, for others their perceived limited drawing ability and the abstract nature of what they were being asked to draw meant that their drawings did not appear to offer any significant additions to their verbal contribution. It is therefore important to note that whilst the drawings provided another layer to the data collection they were seen as integral to the conversation – of the moment – constructed alongside the spoken words and in the context of the interview.

(Austin, 2014, p58)

Researchers in primary school settings can employ a variety of elicitation techniques in addition to those mentioned already. Some ideas you might consider for your research include the following:

- **Problem setting** The researcher might present a problem for a class or a group to solve. Group interactions could be observed and the resulting children's work analysed. The researcher could also interview the children about their perceptions of the task and how they went about solving it.

- **Story** A focus group discussion might begin with a story. A member of the group, other than the researcher, could be invited to read the story. This might help with the power balance in the room and support the children in feeling confident about speaking within the group.

- **Personification of concepts** Children might be given a set of pictures and asked to associate their perception about a particular concept to a picture; adults could be given a topic area and asked to think of a person/thing within that topic that relates to their perception of the concept.

- **Talk objects** You might provide a group with an unfamiliar historical artefact and observe their discussions as they discuss its possible purpose.

Example from practice

Pahl (2009) used artefacts in the form of panorama boxes for her research which examined the relationship between children's talk in the classroom and their multimodal texts. Children created these from shoe boxes to represent an environment such as the ocean or a jungle. The teacher's aim *in setting up this activity was to promote collaborative talk within the classroom, and enhance opportunities for children to make decisions about their meaning-making in small groups* (2009, p189).

If you decide to employ an elicitation technique such as the examples above, you will need to consider the strengths and weaknesses of the technique you intend to use and how you will administer the method in an ethical way which ensures that the participants feel positive about the outcome of the experience. You will need to do this with reference to the specific context of the chosen setting. In her report, Pahl explains the ethical decisions and actions she took about the administration of the research. These include giving the children tape-recorders and digital cameras on their table which they were able to switch on or off when they wished. She also explains that most of the photographs were taken by the children and that she was frequently recorded by the pupils.

Things to think about

1. What evidence do you have that you have chosen a research method that is appropriate for the context and relevant for the intended purpose?

2. Are there skills that you need to develop in order to use the tool efficiently and ethically?

3. How will you administer the technique to ensure the participants have a positive outcome from the experience?

4. What are the limitations and strengths of your chosen approach?

5. Having read the chapter, what advice would you give Maria about her proposed research methods?

References

Austin, R (2014) Figuring out peer group hierarchies in secondary school. Unpublished doctoral thesis available online at: http://etheses.whiterose.ac.uk/6799/ (accessed 7 December 2015).

Bakx, A, Koopman, M, de Kruijf, J and den Brok, P (2015) Primary school pupils' views of characteristics of good primary school teachers: An exploratory, open approach for investigating pupils' perceptions, *Teachers and Teaching theory and practice*, 21: 543–64.

Barton, KC (2015) Elicitation techniques: Getting people to talk about ideas they don't usually talk about, *Theory & Research in Social Education*, 43(2): 179–205.

BBC (n.d.) *Yes Minister*, BBC. Available at: www.bbc.co.uk/comedy/yesminister/ (accessed November 2015).

Bell, A (2007) Designing and testing questionnaires for children, *Journal of Research in Nursing*. 12(5): 461–69.

Bell, J (2010) *Doing Your Research Project*. Milton Keynes: Open University Press.

Broadhead, P, Howard, J and Wood, EA (eds) (2010) *Play and Learning in the Early Years: From Research to Practice*. London: SAGE.

Coates, E and Coates, A (2006) Young children talking and drawing, *International Journal of Early Years Education*, 14(3): 221–41.

Cohen, L, Manion, L and Morrison, C (2013) *Research Methods in Education*. London: Routledge.

Denzin, NK and Lincoln, YS (eds) (1998) *Strategies of Qualitative Inquiry*. Thousand Oaks, CA: SAGE Publications.

Denscombe, M (2010) *Good Research Guide For Small-scale Social Research Projects*. Maidenhead: McGraw Hill.

Jarvis, P., (2010) Born to play: The biocultural roots of rough and tumble play, and its impact upon young children's learning and development. *Play and learning in the early years*, pp. 61–77.

King, N and Horrocks, C (2010) *Interviews in Qualitative Research*. London: SAGE Publications.

McNiff, J and Whitehead, J (2010) *You and Your Action Research Project*. Oxford: Routledge.

Pahl, K (2009) Interactions, intersections and improvisations: Studying the multimodal texts and classroom talk of six- to seven-year-olds, *Journal of Early Childhood Literacy*, 9(2): 188–210.

Saçkes, M, Flevares, LM and Trundle, KC (2010) Four- to six-year-old children's conceptions of the mechanism of rainfall, *Early Childhood Research Quarterly*, 25(4): 536–46.

Further reading

Arthur, J, Waring, M, Coe, R and Hedges, LV (2013) *Research Methods and Methodologies in Education*. London: SAGE.

Kvale, S (2007) *Doing Interviews*. London: SAGE.

MacDonald, A (2012) Young children's photographs of measurement in the home, *Early Years*, 32(1): 71–85.

Newby, P (2014) *Research Methods for Education*. Harlow: Pearsons.

Punch, K (2014) *Introduction to Research Methods in Education*. London: SAGE.

Roberts , H (2014) *Doing Your Early Years Research Project*. London: SAGE.

Rose, G (2012). *Visual Methodologies: An Introduction to Researching with Visual Materials*. London: SAGE.

Chapter 7

Data analysis

Kristy Howells and Peter Gregory

Objectives

This chapter:

- helps you make sense of the data that you have collected;
- guides you through the analysis process within your chosen data collection method;
- suggests ways of presenting your findings.

Chapter summary

Working out what your data has to say will be the way in which you formulate arguments and ideas about what you are researching – and the answers can be both affirming and challenging for your beliefs and practices in primary schools.

Introduction

In the previous chapter, Wendy Cobb explained how to collect your data through interviews and questionnaires, with teachers and/or pupils, and also how to make use of observations and artefacts. This chapter deals with arguably the most exciting part of your research investigation – finding the answers to your research questions by making sense of the data you have collected. You can think of this process as being similar to a game of *Catchphrase*. *Catchphrase* was a television game show which first aired in the 1980s. Contestants would be shown a screen in which a picture depicting a phrase or saying was slowly revealed and they had to buzz in to say what they thought the phrase or saying was as soon as they could work it out. This slow revealing process is similar to what happens when you start to explore what your data has to tell you and the pieces of the puzzle fall into place. Your prize will be the answers you uncover! At this stage in the research process it is not unusual to be feeling anxious that you have collected too much or too little data or that your data is simply not focused or clear enough. The key is not to panic – just think *Catchphrase*. If you spread out all the data, look at it systematically and in detail, and reflect on what you see before you, thinking about how it all fits together, you will be able to understand what you have found out and how this relates to the questions you have asked.

What is your data?

Your first, practical task is to sort and store your data so that it is organised and accessible. Everything needs to be clearly labelled with names, dates and the context in which the data was collected – whether your data consists of electronic audio files, handwritten notes or A2 poster collages. As soon as you can, make the data as unidentifiable as possible – through the use of pseudonyms or labels such as 'Child A', removal of school names and logos or other identifying features – although it is wise to keep a note somewhere to remind you of the original names. At this early stage you might want to make sure you are storing certain sets of data together. For some projects it might be useful to keep all the 'before' and 'after' data separate, whereas for others you might want to organise your data by participant.

Interview transcripts

Interviews, audio or video, require some further consideration here. Transcribing interviews can be seen as the first stage of the analysis process because how you represent what people said requires some kind of interpretation. When you transcribe, you will need to make decisions such as the following.

- Will I transcribe verbatim, including hesitations, repetitions and false starts?

- Will I include emphases where I believe the participant has stressed a particular word?

- Will I transcribe elements of non-standard spoken English, dialect and accent, or will I 'translate'. This is particularly relevant when transcribing very young children's talk.

- Will I include my interpretation of the expression or intent of the speaker – for example, by adding adverbs such as 'angrily' or adding description such as 'shifts uncomfortably in his seat'?

- Will I use punctuation to interpret the speaker's words?

- Will I paraphrase more succinctly where the speaker has 'rambled'?

- Will I include off-topic discussion?

If you are using a formal structured approach in your analysis such as discourse analysis you will find very detailed guidance about transcription of dialogue, but for the purposes of small-scale projects you are likely to use more informal approaches.

The process of transcribing sets the interpretive process in motion. What you perceive as anger might have been the participant being upset – you might interpret someone shifting in their seat as a sign they are uncomfortable with what they have said, but they might just have had a bit of cramp! You cannot avoid this kind of interpretation but you cannot present it completely neutrally either because that is equally misleading.

The response 'Yes I think so' could be transcribed in all the following ways – each way presents a very different interpretation.

- 'Yeah. I think so.'

- 'Yes! I think so!'

- 'Yes . . . I think . . . I think so . . . '

- (Looking puzzled) ' . . . yes (shaking head) . . . I think so' (smiles).

You need to represent what was said, as you see it, to the best of your ability. As we have said throughout this book, you need to be aware of and up-front about all the elements of the research and its writing up that have affected the findings, and this is just another example of where you need to be aware of you, the researcher, in your project.

In a small-scale project you do not need to transcribe all of every interview, as long as you have listened to them many times and become familiar with them. You can expect to take up to 30 minutes to transcribe just five minutes of a one-to-one interview – longer if it is a group interview. This just might not be good use of your time when you are working to a deadline. You can simply transcribe certain sections on which you want to focus in your analysis and write-up. You will need to decide what is best for your context. If you are unsure, consult with your tutor or supervisor.

Writing about your data

The first part of your research project, up to and including the methodology, could be written before you even collect your data. Of course, this might depend on timescales, your own approach to the research and other factors. However, the chapter you cannot possibly write in advance is the data section. There are two parts to this: presentation or reporting of data and analysis of data. Sometimes these two elements are completely separate, but it is more common in small-scale research projects such as yours to intertwine the two. You do need to be aware, however, when you are writing about your data, where you are reporting what you found and where you are analysing it. For example, you might tell your reader that you found out that only 26 per cent of the children in your class attend extra-curricular sports activities. This is interesting, but not analysis. Your analysis asks why this might be, and you might need to draw on other elements of your data in order to answer this question. This is the work that you are doing as you 'interrogate' your data. You do not, in your data section or the associated appendices, present your reader with all the raw data you have collected. Your reader does not need to see every single questionnaire, a transcript of every interview, your detailed observation notes. If you submit all the raw data to your reader you are, in effect, asking them to do the analysis for you. You will be presenting your understanding, your analysis, of the data and to do that you might need only to present to your reader the graphs which show the collated questionnaire data, short transcripts of sections of interviews and a sample of the drawings. You should think of it as explaining your findings to your reader, not just telling them what you found.

Your data analysis section or chapter needs to demonstrate that you have taken a thoughtful and systematic approach to uncovering what your data tells you. If you just take one or two quotes from an interview, one or two instances from your observations or use only one drawing because it stands out to you in some way, this is just 'cherry picking' and leaves you open to accusations of researcher bias. If you went into your research expecting (or hoping) to see something and you take a superficial sweep of your data, you are very likely to see what you want to see. By stepping back and going through a more rigorous and detached process of analysis you allow yourself to be more open to seeing the unexpected and having your initial assumptions challenged.

Being systematic

Stenhouse's (1975) definition of research as *systematic enquiry made public* is key at the analysis stage. It is what makes research distinct from a knee-jerk or unconsidered response to a set of information or findings.

In order to analyse your data you need to get to know it really well. If you have undertaken interviews, listen to the recordings or read the transcripts as many times as you can – at first with an open mind and then with a different focus each time as you become aware of emerging themes or responses – that is, things that keep coming up (or are persistently not mentioned). If you have questionnaires, look at the data in lots of different ways and consider different combinations of responses, comparing answers to different questions and looking for significant discrepancies or similarities. You will need to visit and revisit observation notes, children's drawings, models and artefacts so that you look beyond the surface to some of the revealing details which lie beneath.

Working systematically through your data includes the following.

- Looking for frequency of occurrence of, for example, behaviours, expressions of viewpoint or use of drawn representations.

- Looking for patterns, surprises, the expected, the unexpected. Can they all be identified in the data? If not, why not? If they can, to what extent across all your sample?

- Noticing what is missing from the data. Is there something significant which you might have expected to see which hasn't appeared?

- Reflect on the patterns and themes you have identified. Are there other ways of looking at them? Does a pattern of contradictory statements in an interview context actually reflect the interactions between just two participants?

- Talking to others about what you think you are finding out. See what they say. Rehearse your arguments about why you think you have found what you have.

- Return frequently to the research question(s). Has it/have they been answered? If not, why not? If it has, what is your evidence base for being confident?

- Consider how your findings fit with what you discussed in the literature review. Do you need to go back and add or remove sections so that you are able to make links between your findings and what has already been discovered?

Finding a starting point

A systematic approach to the data is likely to take either a grounded approach or draw on an existing analytic framework. A grounded approach, as described in Chapter 5, examines your data en masse and recurrent aspects are identified, such as the emerging themes in interviews or drawings or observed behaviours. These themes are generated from the data itself, so you might look at interview transcripts and identify every time that teachers refer to the New Curriculum for Science or you might identify where children have used gender stereotyping in their drawings. These might then be further refined as you examine and re-examine your data. So it might be that you look for specific aspects of the science curriculum which are mentioned or particular elements of gender stereotyping. This sort of approach can be applied very systematically by adopting a system of codes and subcodes. However, this might not be appropriate in a small-scale context.

If, however, you are using an existing framework for analysis you will use codes or themes which have been applied to different data sets in similar research and see how they apply to yours. This can sometimes result in the adaptation of the themes to better fit what your data, in your context, is telling you. Drawing on and replicating an existing research project both methodologically and in the analysis process should not be seen as 'cheating'. It is an extraordinarily valuable way of extending findings from one context to others. For small-scale research projects (as well as larger ones), this is often a very good way to begin as you are able to draw on the expertise of others, yet still offer your own interpretation and analysis of *your* data in *your* context.

Example from practice

Braid and Finch (2015) undertook a small-scale study exploring how children responded to picture book read-alouds. They explain, in the abstract, how they used existing research as a framework for analysis but refined and developed it in order to better understand the data that they had collected.

The authors created a framework for analysing the responses, adapting the model of Lawrence Sipe (2008) with its five categories of literacy understanding, by expanding

(Continued)

(Continued)

> on the analytical category to enable a finer analysis of the response. This article discusses the children's depth of thinking and the understandings they developed as they engaged with the read-aloud. It also describes how the adapted framework allowed a closer analysis of these understandings, including the way the elements of art used in the illustrations contributed to the children's ideas. The findings suggest ways picturebooks can be used to promote children's thinking and how teachers can guide discussion about a complex text. Implications for use of the framework in further research are discussed.
>
> (Braid and Finch, 2015, p115)

Being systematic: coding

If you choose to use codes you will need to consider how they can be applied to the form and amount of data you have collected. What are these codes and how can you be sure they are appropriate for your study? As mentioned earlier, in your reading of other published research you may find the authors explain the codes they used. This can be helpful and you can then apply the same ones. Sometimes you will need to build them yourself and it is important as you do so that you discuss them with others so they can comment on your choices and provoke you to think about other possibilities. What you see might be quite different from what others see and another pair of eyes and someone else's analytical insights can be very useful. If you are doing your research as part of a written assignment it is a good idea to use a peer as a critical friend and support each other in the initial thoughts you have about what your data might be revealing.

Example from practice

Gregory (2014) undertook research with primary art co-ordinators. He based part of the nine codings he used on an earlier study by Downing and Watson (2004) as both involved discussing images of art works with teachers and noting their responses, including if they mentioned using the artwork as an example (good or bad) to show pupils, or discussed the content/issue raised or perceived as contained in the artwork or the skill(s) of the artist who had produced the work in the first place. However, in the latter study, Gregory found that more codings were required, which opened up new lines of enquiry and discussion, including the teachers' general ignorance of artworks, their under-confidence and their thinking around making responses to the artworks shown. In this way, it can be seen that the process of revealing the information from which the data can open new challenges for the researcher if the coding adopted is robustly and systematically applied.

Codes can also be applied to interview transcripts, pictures, photographs and video evidence. You will need to think about how you can do this and how you can most effectively present your data.

Example from practice

Below, an extract from a transcribed interview shows how the researcher has highlighted some things which needed further consideration (particularly in the light of published literature already read). The next stage has been to add a number of topic codes to allow the selected text to be pulled together.

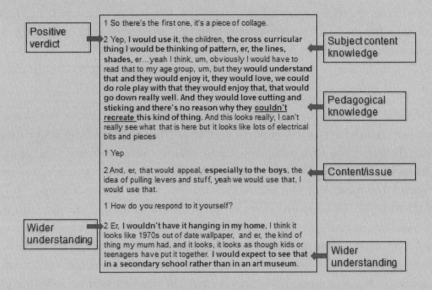

Figure 7.1 Coding interview transcript

From here a comparative table could be constructed to make further comparisons, drawing together into one place all the quotes which seem to relate to each of the topic codes used. From this a further development would be to refine the codes and use them analytically – for example, by posing additional questions and reflecting on the evidence provided to work towards an answer. This is the analytic coding mentioned above. Using this small segment of text above, such a question might be 'Is there any link or correlation between subject content knowledge and pedagogical knowledge?'

Analysis takes time, consideration and reflection. Answers to research questions very rarely jump out at the first reading of raw data (in whichever form): they need to be pursued, checked and double-checked before a researcher (and the reading audience) can be convinced that they have identified issues embedded in the data. You are engaging in an interpretive act. What you see in the data is related to who you are and your own experiences, expertise and understandings. You need to find ways of standing apart from your data as well as engaging in it. Asking what others see when they look at your data can be illuminating and challenging, and can facilitate the recursive process of analysis. Be prepared to look at your data from different perspectives so that you get to see different things – and don't be satisfied with what seems obvious without looking beyond it.

Sharing your data with others

In sharing data that you have analysed, you need to be able to explain it in the simplest and easiest ways possible so everyone will understand exactly what the data shows and how it links to answering the questions. There are a number of ways of presenting and sharing your data depending on the kind of data you have, but do understand that these by themselves may not be the same as analysing the data. It is your job to explain things clearly to the reader, so avoid presenting the data and leaving it to the audience to work out what the analysis actually tells them. As you discuss your data, you will also need to show your reader how it links to the themes you explored in the literature review. You are adding to the stew, so you need to demonstrate that you understand what it is that your findings contribute to the discussions.

As mentioned before, you do *not* present all your raw data to your reader. But as you discuss issues which have arisen, you will need to provide examples from your data to illustrate the points you have made. If you state that 'children often described positive experiences of physical education throughout their schooling', then you need to insert some quotes from your data which show this. It is fine to just present these as you would quotations from literature: in quotation marks, indented and labelled with the child's name (or pseudonym) and the context of the statement – for example, Interview group A 21/10/2015. (You will have explained what 'Interview group A' is in the methodology section.) The citing of evidence from your data is essential – you need to be able to justify your findings. Simply saying 'The children were overwhelmingly positive about reading at home' is not enough. You then need to show your reader how your data shows this. You might, therefore, cite quantitative data: 95 per cent of the children answered 'Yes, very much' to the question 'Do you like to read at home?' or you could use quotes from the children from interviews.

Alternatively, if you felt that the different responses were of interest and revealed different things about your research findings, you could present a number of statements as a table showing responses from different participants.

Where your participants' responses have not been recorded electronically, you need to ensure that your reader knows that you are using field notes or jottings which were made during interviews or observations – and that they are not verbatim. Do not use quotation marks unless you are quoting directly from your participants.

Example from practice

Jarman (2013) undertook a dissertation, for her undergraduate degree, about the benefits of swimming to Key Stage 2 pupils. She presented her data to the reader in the form of a table which collated the answers she had received to the question 'Can you think of a time when you may have seen a child in the swimming pool who did not enjoy curriculum lessons, thrive on learning outside the classroom?'

	Can you think of a time when you may have seen a child in the swimming pool who did not enjoy curriculum lessons, thrive on learning outside the classroom?
A	Happy – because not in the classroom. It is a hands-on activity and not reading and writing. Therefore, they did not feel silly.
B	Poor academically – her face shone.
C	Not all children are Gifted and Talented in the classroom but some excel outside the classroom egg. PE dance, artistic talent. Therefore if they are do well at swimming even Just 25 metres – it is a huge boost for their confidence.
D	A child was distracted in the class but more focused in the swimming pool.
E	Again, a child who found it hard to concentrate in the classroom, but did well in the swimming pool and enjoyed the praise from his teachers.
F	Enjoying the freedom – a real achievement and proud that he had achieved something.
G	On several occasions it has been great to see a child who finds it challenging to work in the classroom, where they enjoy being one of the best.

This data can then be analysed in the text, making reference to different answers or common themes or responses. Labelling the responses (or numbering lines of transcript) is really important.

Sometimes you might want to include a longer quote from a participant which you want to go on to analyse in some depth. In this case, you could present the quote as before, but with quotes of more than ten lines it is helpful to number the lines so that you can refer your reader to specific parts of the quote. For longer quotes, it might be better to put the transcript in an appendix (with numbered lines for ease of reference as before) so that it doesn't break up the flow of the text too much (or eat into your word count).

Example from practice

Mercer et al. (2009) looked at dialogic teaching in primary science. In their research report they present long sections of dialogue, followed by a commentary on each. The commentary gives further contextualising detail and makes some comment on each section. This is the presentation of the data. The analysis of the dialogue is in the next section of their article, which is called 'Results and discussion'. Here they draw common themes together and examine the whats and whys of the results that they have presented to the reader.

Presenting quantitative data

The purpose of a figure such as a graph or pie chart is to show trends, patterns and relationships in your data. This is the best way to present quantitative data. In the discussion text which accompanies the figure, the 'story' that the data shows must be presented and applied. You must not just present the graph and expect your reader to understand its significance. When using graphs and pie charts, it is also important to ensure that, where you have applied a mathematical approach to analysis, the mathematics has been used appropriately. As mentioned in Gill Hope's chapter, if you have only a small number of participants it just doesn't make sense to talk in terms of percentages. If you are looking at discrete data such as frequency of use of subject-specific terminology for each participant, you need to use a graphical representation such as a bar chart. A line graph would not be suitable as this is used to show continuous data – data which changes over time. So, a line graph might be used to show children's engagement with independent reading over the period of half an hour of silent reading time. If you are looking to be able to visually represent the percentages of a whole, a pie chart is the best bet – for example, if you want to show the ways in which children used the role-play area over the period of a whole day in a nursery setting.

There is further reading at the end of the chapter which you can use to develop your understanding of the presentation of quantitative data.

Example from practice

Howells (2012) investigated the contribution of physical education lessons to children's physical activity. The graph below shows the overall mean number of minutes of moderate to vigorous physical activity within the whole school day for all children on days that had physical education lessons and on days that did not have those lessons.

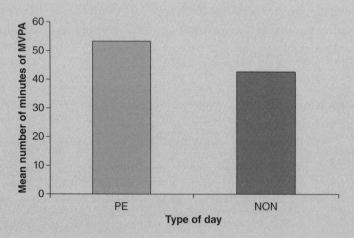

Figure 7.2 Quantitative data graph

This is the most effective, straightforward and helpful way of presenting this data. It is immediately visually obvious what the data is saying and the labelling of the graph is clear to the reader. This data can then be discussed without having to take up valuable word count explaining what the graph can show far more effectively.

Keeping it simple

For both qualitative and quantitative data you might want to use tables to show very specific things about your data – for example, you might look at the same question asked in a questionnaire or interview and compare the answers from different groups, either as numbers or as words. You might compare particular stereotypically gendered features of drawings drawn by boys and girls (this might involve inserting pictures of parts of the drawings or simply listing features). You might look at the different manipulatives children choose to use to work out particular calculations. Presenting these key aspects of your data as a table makes it easier for your reader to follow your arguments when you come to the analysis.

Alternatively, tables can be used to collate elements of your findings where you have undertaken a process of deconstruction of your data. You might have identified specific elements or aspects of, for example, children's observed behaviours, so that instead of simply stating 'looked at a book' you add additional information about the book activity: type of book, length of interaction with the book or time of day that the book reading took place. Again, you are making the data more easily accessible to the reader with key elements highlighted for them.

Example from practice

Cook (2014) undertook a final dissertation for her undergraduate degree about the impact of phonics on improving reading. She used the table below to show the strategies used by a pupil in reading unfamiliar words.

Word	Strategies used
Word 'searched'	Broke word into phonemes – s/ear/ch/ed
Word 'speck'	Used phonics – s/p/e/ck
Word 'computer'	Broke word into several syllables – comp/compu/comp/coper required prompting to finish word
Word 'spots'	Used phonics – s/p/o/t/s
Word 'fall'	Used knowledge of familiar work 'all' – f/all
Word 'together'	Split words into familiar words – to/get/her and then blended word
Word 'sneak'	Used syllable division – sn/eak
Word 'answers'	Used syllables unsuccessfully – anst/er – hesitated and waited to be helped
Word 'powder'	Used phonics and syllable division – p/ow/der

She was then able to refer back to this table a number of times to explain terminology and findings and offer further analysis.

Presenting other forms of data

In the last chapter we discussed other approaches to data and you need to think carefully about the best way of presenting these data forms to your reader.

If you use a figure such as a photo (ones taken by the children or images of artefacts which have been produced as part of your research approach) or a drawing, you need to consider whether further annotations or explanations might be helpful. You might, therefore, include a paragraph after each image which gives a little more contextual detail or draws attention to key aspects. Alternatively, you could label the picture, either with captions or with numbers which you later refer back to.

If you are presenting examples of children's writing or other school work in your data section you need to be very clear about the elements which are pertinent to the research. You will be very familiar with your data but your reader is not, so you must be sure to make it clear which bits are the most relevant and why. Highlighting sections and providing annotations can do this effectively.

You must also have a discussion section which draws together the analysis of the images and what their relevance and importance is in the light of your research question, so that you elucidate the themes and findings that have arisen.

Data panics

Rest assured that no matter what data you have collected, how much you have collected and how often you have looked at it, you will still think that it isn't going to give you the answers you need. All data can tell you something. Whether it tells you anything like what you expected it to is another story!

What if my data doesn't answer my research question?

It is essential to remain focused on your research question as you go through the data analysis – there will be 'red herrings' and possible interesting side-tracks which might distract you, but you have to keep remembering what it was you set out to explore. Your reader needs to know, and will be looking to find out, what the answers were. Ultimately, if your reading audience (or marker) cannot find the answers from your efforts, you will suffer the consequences. You need to have a mind-set which continually rehearses the answers that you are focusing on as you go through the processes of undertaking the analysis.

If you find you cannot convince yourself that the answers can be found, it is possibly because your research skills were not robust enough or even that your research question was not quite right. The first thing to do here is to talk the situation through with your supervising tutor or critical friend. Sometimes an impressive piece of reflective work can result from an honest appraisal of shortcomings or errors of judgement if they are embraced in the analysis and discussion stage. In some instances your tutor may even be able to suggest a better reworking of your research question(s) that link to the information that has been collected. This is perfectly acceptable and can be written about in the analysis section of your project.

It might be, too, that you have simply got lost in the data and need someone to suggest certain paths to follow rather than trying to head in all directions at once! Whatever you do, if you're not sure that the research question(s) have been answered, don't carry on regardless and hope for the best as this only implies that you haven't noticed that the issues exist – research is about a process of exploration and if you got lost along the way you need to be upfront about it – research should demonstrate integrity at every stage.

What if I have too much data?

As you have gone through the planning of your research you have thought carefully about the sorts of data you need to collect in order to focus on finding answers to your question. It is quite usual, however, for new researchers to take a belt-and-braces type approach to data collection and collect far more than is needed. You might have been advised to work with a group of four children but you were worried in case one child was away, or another didn't contribute enough to the discussions, so you decided to work with two groups. Or you collected one set of data which didn't quite seem right, so you collected another set in a different context to 'check' what you were seeing. Don't worry if you feel this is what has happened to you!

Revisit your research question – the first thing you can do is to be ruthless about the data you have collected. If you have collected data that was not directly related to the research question, don't even look at it. If your data is relevant but just seems insurmountable, then you need to start a systematic chunking process. Perhaps you were looking at children's and teachers' perceptions of a particular aspect of practice. If so, you need to sort your data into a pile of children's perceptions to look at first, then look at what the teachers' perceptions say; do not try to do all of this at once. If you looked at 'How do boys vs. girls . . . ?', this immediately gives you a boys' and a girls' chunk of data. Similarly, if you compared key stages, or year groups, you again have chunks of data to start to analyse. With interviews you may feel there is simply too much data to tackle. You don't necessarily have to transcribe all the interviews – just listening to the recording or reviewing your notes is sufficient to start with. Within your data you could look to see whether you have quantitative data that is comparable across many interviews. For example, how often did teachers mention that they were confident in teaching science in the new curriculum? This type of answer could be reported as a percentage or illustrated through a pie chart or figures as discussed previously. The same can be true for questionnaires. It may feel overwhelming that you have asked 14 teachers (the whole school) 10 questions, giving you 140 answers to analyse, but how many closed end questions do you have that you could again turn into pie charts or figures and tables, giving you a basis to begin to question why the answers are as they are. Comparing answers to connected questions might also be useful. For example, if you have asked children what their favourite type of book is and also asked them to list the last three books they have read, this will give you a great way to start thinking about whether the children are reading books which they enjoy (and your analysis will go on to think about why or why not this might be).

You can also take a tightly focused approach to the analysis of the data where you decide to *only* look at a particular theme or idea. For example, you might be particularly interested in children's use of subject-specific vocabulary in science as this has arisen as a key theme, in which case you can look for this and only this in your data. This means that you need only transcribe sections of interview where this is evident or you might be able to focus your analysis on a small section of a questionnaire or other data-collection method. Where you are limited for time (or have a limited word count for an assignment) this is often the best approach to take. Large amounts of data take up a lot of space in terms of simply reporting *what* you have found and might leave you with too little space to get to the nitty gritty of the *why*. You can, in your analysis section, state that you are focusing on one aspect and justify why this is. Other avenues which could have been explored further can be referred to in the conclusion of your research report where you suggest further research and areas for investigation, but in the main you leave them out of your analysis.

What if I have too little data?

However carefully designed your research project is, it might well be the case that unforeseen circumstances occur and children are unexpectedly absent, unexpectedly reticent or unexpectedly unwilling to participate. All of this might mean that you have less data than you had hoped for. As a rule of thumb, it is probably *not* a good idea to compare the amount of data collected with your friends, as it will depend on what you have asked as your question as to what is the 'right' amount. It is perfectly possible to write a whole Master's dissertation on a very small amount of data – less can be more as you are forced to examine the data you have in far greater detail than you can possibly manage when you have large amounts. As before, the first thing to do is to revisit your research question and remind yourself what it was you wanted to find out. If you have asked 'What is the effect of hot-seating children as the villain in traditional tales on their written representation of the character's voice?' you may have only wanted to know the impact of hot-seating on a particular group of children. This is important research as it impacts on *your* understanding and your knowledge of an approach to teaching writing and how you may or may not use it more effectively for this group of children. You are likely, therefore, to have less data than someone who has questioned the benefits of swimming for Key Stage 2 children and observed all pupils in KS2, as well as questioned teachers and parents. As long as you have enough data to give you some answers about some of what you wanted to find out, that is fine!

What if my data tells me interesting, but irrelevant things?

Stand firm! In the process of analysing your data it is not unusual to uncover unexpected findings. If these findings sit within the parameters of your research questions, then these can provide rich and valuable discussion points within your analysis chapter. Go ahead and explore them! However, it is equally likely that your data uncovers completely unrelated issues. You might see a possible parental influence over children's reading choices, for example, but if you were looking at children's responses to subversive picture books, is this relevant or significant? It might just be that several of the children mentioned that 'I'm not allowed to read that book'. This is interesting, but it is not your research project – it is another one entirely. You might, in the conclusion to your research, mention this as a possible further avenue for investigation, but you must not allow yourself to be distracted from your own focus.

What if my data isn't good quality?

This is an interesting question. What counts as 'good quality' data is questionable. As we have already said, a very small amount of data can lead to a rich and detailed discussion. Not getting the data you wanted or expected is a discussion in itself. In the hot-seating example above, if you do not see any evidence of the impact of the hot-seating on children's writing, that is your finding, and you can write about why that might be. Perhaps the research design or implementation was a factor, but perhaps it is the case that hot-seating *doesn't* have a significant or identifiable effect on writing in the data you collected. If your carefully worded questions in a semi-structured interview did not elicit the responses you needed, you can examine why this is in your analysis. Perhaps the children were worried about appearing critical and therefore gave only positive responses. If this is the case, there is much to be discussed about why this might be. That is the focus of your analysis. Sometimes what is *not* said is even more revealing than what is. If children's drawings were rushed, unfinished, lacking in detail, this might tell you something about the way you approached the explanation of the task. It might tell you something about the children's drawing skills. It might tell you something about this method of data collection – it just wasn't appropriate! Again, this becomes a focus for discussion in itself. You analyse what you can from the data but you also discuss the reasons why the method didn't seem to work. It might simply have been that you were required to collect data in too short a timescale in an inappropriate context and without the opportunity to try alternative approaches. All of this thinking, this analysis, is good. You can write about all of this, demonstrating your reflective, analytical, critical engagement with the research process. Research which doesn't achieve what it set out to do still serves a purpose in the research 'stew', which was discussed in the Introduction.

Keeping it in perspective

The data you have collected can tell you very interesting things, but keep in mind that it is only generalisable to the group of children you have investigated, the setting and the time period in which it was collected. Your findings are unlikely to change the world (even though you might want them to). You are investigating and questioning current practice and at times that is your practice and no one else's.

It is essential to avoid any grand claims or to suggest that you have 'proved' something to be the case. Throughout this section (and in your conclusion) you should be careful to write in a tentative, cautious way. This is discussed in the next chapter, too, as we think about your academic 'voice' in your writing. You will be saying, 'It might be. . . '; 'Perhaps it is the case that . . . '; 'It seems to be that . . . '. Small-scale projects especially offer an insight into a particular way of doing at a particular point in time and in a particular context. You will have found out something about something – something valuable and worthwhile but very likely only applicable within a very small circle of influence.

Throughout your analysis you need to keep your literature review in mind. You will have already examined what existing research has to say about the area that you are investigating. A significant part of the analysis section is how you weave together your findings with the existing research you have already discussed. So if others have said that children's jottings are significant in their ability to solve mathematical problems and your findings say something similar, you will be able to draw on those other findings alongside your own. Sometimes you might feel that your research is saying something different, or opening up new avenues. It is important at this point to remember that your research is small scale and local, so that a tentative voice is crucial. If your findings from six children appear different from a published study which worked with sixty children you should use your analysis section to question why that might be before tentatively suggesting that what you have found might be significant and worth further investigation.

Have I got it right?

When you present and analyse your data the most important thing is to draw together findings from across your data. If you present each part of your data separately and discuss it separately, you have only done half the job. The process of analysis, the *Catchphrase* bit, is to understand how all the parts fit together to make a whole. In the discussion and analysis section it is usually far better to present your findings as key themes which refer to your data across the piece than to go through each piece of data you have collected one by one.

What does it all mean?

Miles and Huberman (1994, p12) helpfully set out the flow of activity in data analysis. Having collected the data in the study, there is naturally propulsion towards the drawing of conclusions as a direct consequence of the 'story' contained in the data. However, it is a mistake to believe that this is a simple linear progression as they argue that when a rigorous analytic process is undertaken there may be several cycles of considered investigation of that data before any such conclusions can be drawn and defended. They refer to the activities of 'data display' and 'data reduction'. We have tried to demonstrate these as the creation of tables or figures which both help to present the information gathered, and then as a means of interrogating the data further and allowing even deeper understanding and analysis to be undertaken. This process in turn may drive the researcher back to consider other ways of presenting information, changing codings or defined themes a number of times before satisfying themselves that the 'story' can indeed be justified and presented (or discussed) in such a way as to convince others. This is not a quick-fix mechanism but takes time and careful application of the principles of sound research.

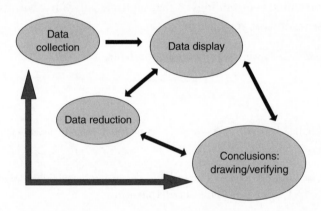

Figure 7.3   Components of data analysis from Miles and Huberman (1994)

Depending on the forms of data collected, you need to develop your confidence in creating overviews of your findings. These can provide helpful stepping stones in the development of your thinking and questioning processes. You ought to work to your own strengths by recognising your own learning styles – for example, do you respond better to visual representations than to lists of text? Remember you may choose to construct a table or chart so you can 'see' the bigger picture of your study or you may work by spreading your papers across the floor or building an Excel spreadsheet.

Conclusion

This chapter has discussed ways of making sense of the data collected. By adopting a systematic approach, the gradual revealing process can be used to good effect to identify issues, themes and trends. This in turns will allow a clear presentation of the 'story' contained in the data so that others can appreciate what you have found out.

The next chapter will consider the importance of adopting high standards of academic writing and applying a rigorous approach through your study which can be defended when interrogated by other readers.

Things to think about

1. What is your research question? Have you answered it? If not, have you explained why?

2. What are the most important things you have learned from your data?

3. Have you worked systematically through all the relevant data and not just gone with first impressions?

4. Have you presented your findings so that someone unfamiliar with your research can make sense of what you have found?

5. Have you *analysed* as well as presented your data?

References

Braid, C and Finch, B (2015) "Ah, I know why . . . ": Children developing understandings through engaging with a picture book, *Literacy*, 49(3): 115–22.

Cook, E (2014) What impact does phonics have to improve reading? (unpublished dissertation). BA Primary Education, 7–11, Canterbury Christ Church University.

Downing, D and Watson, R (2004). *School Art: What's in It?* Slough: NFER.

Gregory, P (2014) An investigation into the contribution made by primary art coordinators to the development of the teaching of art: the evolution of identities, understanding and practice (unpublished Ed. D. thesis), University of Greenwich.

Howells, K (2012) Using accelerometers and Qwizdom to measure the physical activity levels of primary aged children. Presented at the International Convention on Science, Education and Medicine in Sport (ICSEMIS). July, Glasgow.

Jarman, D (2013) The benefits of swimming to a Key Stage 2 pupil (unpublished dissertation). BA Primary Education, 7–11, Canterbury Christ Church University.

Mercer, N, Dawes, L and Staarman, JK (2009) Dialogic teaching in the primary science classroom. *Language and Education*, 23(4): 353–69.

Miles, M and Huberman, M (1994) *Qualitative Data Analysis: An Expanded Sourcebook*. London: SAGE.

Stenhouse, L (1975) *An Introduction to Curriculum Research and Development*. London: Heinemann.

Further reading

Denzin, NK and Lincoln, Y (eds) (2005) *The Sage Handbook of Qualitative Research*. London: Sage.

Gee, J (2010) *How to do Discourse Analysis: A Toolkit*. London: Routledge.

Gibbs, G (2008) *Analysing Qualitative Data*. London: SAGE.

Punch, K (2009) *Introduction to Research Methods in Education*. London: SAGE.

Silverman, D (2001) *Interpreting Qualitative Data: Methods for Analysing Talk, Text and Interaction*. London: SAGE.

Chapter 8

Academic writing: how do I write it up?

Viv Wilson

Objectives

This chapter:

- explains what we mean by 'academic writing' and the associated conventions;
- explains the need for careful referencing;
- considers the audience and purpose for your writing.

Chapter summary

Academic writing is a discipline which follows certain rules which must be followed so that you can demonstrate your understanding and make your contribution to the world of educational research.

Introduction

By this stage of your education you probably have a fair idea of what we might mean when we talk about 'academic writing'. It is likely that you will have been introduced to some of the issues associated with the practice of writing in academic contexts, such as the concept of plagiarism and the use of academic referencing. This chapter is not going to cover these topics in detail again. Instead, it will concentrate on how academic writing 'works' and how you might be able to use that understanding to improve or develop your own academic writing skills.

Academic writing, like other kinds of writing (plays, poems, emails, texts, etc.) operates within a social context and, as with all social contexts, there are rules, often unspoken, that apply. These rules are much more than using correct academic referencing conventions, important though these are. The rules involve the use of particular forms of grammar, particular choices of vocabulary and the avoidance of personal or 'informal' language. For quite a few people entering higher education, this type of writing is difficult and off-putting. So why do universities and the world of educational research generally think it is important, and why do they insist that you learn to write in this way?

A key purpose of a university education, and of the educational research associated with university-level study, is that of the development of new knowledge and insight. In order to convey this, writing needs to be clear, well ordered and above all *believable*. The writer (you!) needs to convince the reader of their claims by substantiating key points with evidence, and taking different points into consideration. The form of writing known as 'academic' writing has developed in order to do just this.

'57 varieties' of academic writing

There is not just one kind of writing which is used within university contexts. Different subject disciplines use writing conventions in different ways, so that writing an English or history assignment is very different from writing a scientific report. Both kinds of writing are regarded as forms of academic writing within their subject disciplines.

As someone involved in studying teaching, it is very likely that you will have been asked to write in different ways as part of your own professional development; for example, you may have been asked to write reflectively about your own experiences in schools. This type of writing is recognised as an important aspect of professional learning, with its own expectations about how you write and the kinds of things you write about. You will already know that this kind of writing is very different from the kind of writing you are expected to use when you write an assignment which asks you to 'discuss' an idea in education. Writing up your research will involve you in using several different kinds of writing in the process of making your own 'contribution to knowledge'. You will need to *describe* your research context; you will need to *explain* how you collected your information; you will need to write *critically and analytically* to discuss the research literature which informs your study and also to discuss the findings of your own investigation. Taken overall, you will be developing an argument which supports your own claim to knowledge: the different kinds of writing will work together to enable this to happen.

Presenting and structuring your research writing

If you have been working your way through this book as you prepare to undertake your own educational research project, you will probably have been reading research articles about the area of your own investigation. As well as helping you locate your own work alongside that of others (see Chapter 4), this will also be preparing you to understand the ways in which educational research is usually written up.

Although there is not a standard pattern for writing educational research, as there is for scientific lab reports, there are key elements we would expect to see. The subheadings used in research articles are not always the same, and sometimes two or more of these elements may be combined in a single section, but they are pretty consistently present in one form or another.

If you are writing up your research as part of a formal university programme, you will probably have been given specific guidance on what to include, but the following list covers the usual elements. It is not coincidental that these are also reflected in the chapters in this book.

- *The abstract* – usually a brief summary of the research, including reference to the research approach, methods and main findings.

- *An introduction* – this often outlines the significance of the main research question.

- *The context in which the research took place* – sometimes included in the research methods section.

- *The academic context* – 'the 'literature review' which locates the research within the current field of knowledge.

- The *research approach* taken, the specific *research methods* used and the *approach to data analysis*.

- *The findings* from the research study, following analysis of the data. How these are presented will depend on the type of data collected.

- *Discussion of the findings,* where the results of the research are interpreted, in the light of other research findings.

- *Conclusions*, which may also include recommendations for future practice, depending on the key purpose of the research study.

Example from practice

Experienced research writers sometimes interpret this structure fairly freely, but the essential components are always present in published research. The following chart indicates how these elements appear in two very different research articles, the first by MacClure et al. (2012) which examines how young children acquire a reputation for 'problematic behaviour' in school, and the second, by Webster and Blatchford (2015), which examines the nature and quality of the experiences of pupils with statements of special educational needs (SEN) in mainstream schools.

	MacClure et al. (2012)	Webster and Blatchford (2015)
Abstract	Outlines the research focus question and key thematic findings.	Outlines the research focus, the research methods and the key thematic findings.
Introduction	Outlines the research question: how young children acquire a reputation for 'problematic behaviour' in school.	Provides background to the key focus – the role of Teaching Assistants (TAs) in supporting pupils with SEN. Refers to previous research showing that the pupils working mainly with TAs have a more limited educational experience than their peers and make relatively less progress.
Research context	Briefly described in the Introduction and again in the 'Research outline' section.	
Literature review	Brief discussion of the problem of 'behaviour' in school, followed by a longer outline of the theoretical framework used to interpret the classroom observations.	Next section identifies two research questions: the nature and quality of pupils' experiences and the management of this provision.
Research approach, methods, approach to data analysis	Titled 'Outline of the research': short description of schools involved, use of ethnographic approach, use of analytical framework as described in literature review.	Titled 'Methodology', this is a very detailed explanation of the research approach (48 pupil case studies) including sampling, observations in schools, interviews and examination of paperwork. The 48 case studies were analysed to identify key themes.
Findings	Findings presented in thematic sections with discussion and links to other literature in each section. Examples of teacher–pupil dialogue given to support the thematic analysis.	The four key themes are presented in detail, supported by quotations and other evidence from the case studies.
Discussion		Discussion of the findings is separate from the findings themselves. Links are made to other research conducted by the authors.
Conclusions	Titled 'Implications' in this article.	Titled 'Implications for policy and practice' in this article. A fairly lengthy section, including references to other literature.*
Notes	*Generally, we would advise you not to include new literature references in the concluding sections of your research report. In this case, the authors are effectively locating their literature review at the end of the article because this is part of a series of articles around the same topic.	

The following is another way to think about the research process, as it is expressed in the writing up.

- What is the problem or question I am concerned with? (Introduction)

- Why is it important and what have other people said/found out about it? (Literature review)

- What information did I need to answer my question and how did find it? (Context, research approach, methods, analysis)

- What did I find? (Findings)

- What do I think this means in terms of my research question? (Discussion, conclusions, implications)

Using your skills in academic writing will enable you to link these key elements together to develop a clear, integrated account of your own research investigation. The following sections of this chapter take a closer look at ways of developing and improving your own academic writing.

Structuring your writing: connecting ideas and paragraphs

The process of linking ideas in your research writing is very important for you to develop your claim to knowledge. The structure discussed above is part of the process, but you need to be working at the level of paragraphs, and even sentences, in order to communicate your research clearly. To do this, you will need a clear idea of the sequence of ideas you want to write about in each section.

How you arrive at this sequence is up to you – there is no one 'right' way to do this, no matter what you may have been told at earlier stages of your education. For some people, it is vital to have an outline before they start writing, but for others arriving at the best sequence of ideas emerges later. Fortunately, the ability to cut and paste in word processing makes it easy to move sections of text around, and much of this chapter was written using this approach. What is important is for you to know what approach to writing suits you best and for you to organise your time appropriately. If you are a 'planner' you will need to spend longer on the preparatory process to get all your ideas in order, but if you are a 'diver', you will need to allow plenty of time to reorganise the first (and second and third) drafts of your writing.

Paragraphing

Each paragraph in your research writing should develop one theme or idea, and the theme of one paragraph should link with that of the next in some way. Where you are moving on to a completely different set of ideas or a new section of your writing, a subheading can be used to make this clear to the reader.

A paragraph can be thought of as an essay in miniature: there is an introduction, sometimes called the 'topic sentence', followed by supporting information. These usually provide explanations and/or evidence to support the key theme of the paragraph, although sometimes contrasting ideas can also be included. In a longer paragraph, a concluding sentence is also helpful to the reader, drawing the ideas together. Refer back to the analysis of the paragraph from Hallam and Parsons (2013) in Chapter 4 for an example.

Spending time to clarify your topic sentences can be very helpful. They can form the basis of your writing plan, or alternatively you can list them to check that you have organised your paragraphs in the best order.

Connectives

The use of connectives, or 'signalling words', helps to create the flow or cohesion of ideas within each paragraph. These connectives can show connections: 'in addition', ' furthermore'); or contrast: ('however', 'although'); they can indicate relationship: 'consequently', 'therefore', and summarise: 'finally', 'in summary'. There are many lists of such words available – for example, in Gillett et al., 2009, p105) and you will find it useful to have such a list available while you are writing, to enable you to select the most precise connectives for your purposes as you construct your paragraphs.

Connectives can also sometimes be used to connect paragraphs in the same section of academic writing, although usually you will need to make links between paragraphs using longer sentences. Linking key words or ideas from one paragraph to the next also helps to ensure that the reader can follow the flow of your argument. Look at the following extract to analyse the different ways in which connections are made within and between the two paragraphs. A commentary is provided at the end of this chapter.

Example from practice

The Zombie Stalking English Classrooms: Social Class and Educational Equality (Reay, 2006, pp291–2)

The prevailing fallacy for much of the past two decades has been that schools can make all the difference necessary. The school effectiveness and improvement movement was hegemonic long enough to have a number of lasting effects (Schostak, 2000). The focus was to be on teachers and within school, and particularly within classroom processes. If we can only make teachers good enough and equip them with sufficient skills and competencies, then the wider social context of schooling is seen as unimportant. The contemporary 'wisdom' has been that teaching and learning is improved by concentrating almost entirely on concerns about teachers' subject knowledge and pupil performance, both of which are seen to be desituated (Macdonald, 2000). On one hand, this has been a paradoxical process of surveillance and prescription in which teachers have been reduced to technicians and divested much of their earlier scope for autonomy and initiative in relation to pedagogy and curriculum, and on the other investing them with impossible powers of transforming educational failure into success without any of the knowledge and understanding that is necessary before they can even begin to make a small headway into an enormous problem.

In contrast, Pat Mahony and Ian Hextall's (2000) insightful analysis shows that the complex relationships and practices inside schools and classrooms require knowledges, approaches and a reflexivity that goes far beyond the skills and competencies approach

(Continued)

> *(Continued)*
>
> to teacher training. Teachers do not simply deliver the National Curriculum and enact a positive discipline policy; they also confront contextual circumstances such as dilemmas over levels and distribution of resources, acts of violence and aggression, complex patterns of interpersonal and group relationships, power struggles for control and dominance, disputes over achievement, and issues about what constitutes 'really useful knowledge' for different groups of students. All these multifaceted dilemmas facing teachers are imbued with gender, ethnicity and social class.

It is important to take time to connect the sentences within each paragraph around a single theme and to make clear connections between paragraphs. This enables the reader to understand your overall argument.

While the structure of your research report and the structure of the paragraphs within the different sections is extremely important, there are some other aspects of your academic writing which also require attention. The next sections consider these in more detail.

Bigger is always better – right?

If you think that academic writing requires lots of big words and lengthy sentences, you may need to think again. Academic writing should be clear, logical and accurate. This does mean that vocabulary choice is important, so that you select words whose meaning is as precise as possible in order to communicate your ideas. However, this does not mean that you need to over-complicate things by using more words than you need, or by choosing more elaborate alternatives. Try reading the following sentence from the Plain English Campaign and explaining what it means: 'High quality learning environments are a necessary pre-condition for the facilitation and enhancement of the on-going learning process.' It can be simplified as: 'Children need good schools if they are to learn properly.'

Don't be fooled into thinking that long words and long sentences automatically make your writing better or more 'academic'.

Formal writing conventions

We have already indicated that there are conventions which govern academic writing and which enable the reader to recognise a piece of writing as 'academic', as opposed to some other writing form. These can be divided into two main areas: the use of formal language and language structures in your writing and that of writing 'critically'. We will discuss these two areas separately for the moment but, as you will see, effective 'critical' writing uses many formal language structures. However, not all formal writing is necessarily critical.

Formal writing avoids the use of colloquial language

In formal writing, we would use the words 'pupils' or 'children' rather than 'kids'. Similarly, it avoids the use of contractions (can't, won't, wouldn't) and writes the words out in full (cannot, will not, would not). The exception to this convention is where we are directly quoting someone's speech – for example, as part of an interview.

Wherever possible, aim to avoid using verb phrases such as 'carried out', 'find out', 'looked into'. These are very commonly used in speech, but are a bit too informal for academic writing. Here are some alternative examples we could use in a summary of research which might be part of a literature review (see Chapter 4).

Less formal	More formal
They carried out an investigation	They conducted an investigation
They wanted to find out . . .	They wanted to discover . . .
They looked into whether . . .	They investigated whether . . .
They needed to think about different research methods	They needed to consider different research methods
In this essay I will look at . . .	In this essay I will discuss/consider/explore . . .

Formal writing sometimes uses the passive voice

This form of expression makes the object of a sentence into the subject and concentrates attention on an action or a result, rather than on the person carrying the action out, as shown in the examples in the table below.

Active voice	Passive voice
They conducted an investigation.	An investigation was conducted.
I needed to consider different research methods.	Different research methods were considered.
We interviewed 40 primary teachers.	40 primary teachers were interviewed.

In these examples, it is the investigation, the research methods and the primary teachers that are important, rather than the people carrying out the research activities. Using the passive voice can create variety in your writing, and avoid the over-use of words such as 'they' where you are outlining the work of others. However, you will need to make it clear whose research you are discussing through the use of accurate referencing.

Some writers also use the passive voice to describe their own research, as in two of the examples above, in order to avoid using the 'first person' (I, we) too often. Opinions about the use of the first person in academic writing vary, as we shall see later in this chapter, but so too do opinions about the use of the passive voice. The passive voice can create an impression of scientific objectivity which you might think adds an air of authority to writing, but it can also make your meaning less clear and alienate your reader. In a small-scale study such as the investigation you are likely to carry out, it can also sound pretentious.

Formal writing usually avoids emotive or subjective language

One reason that the use of the first person might be frowned upon is that it sometimes indicates a personal opinion which is not based on considered evidence. Phrases such as 'in my opinion', 'I think' or 'I believe' are very rarely used in academic writing and are best avoided.

Similarly, you should be very careful of emotive language in your discussion. This is language that clearly indicates your personal opinion, even if you don't use 'I' in your writing. Examples might include words such as 'luckily', 'unfortunately', 'surprisingly'.

Formal writing avoids the use of direct or rhetorical questions and exclamations

'So why do many students have difficulties with academic writing? Surely it is easy to learn?' This sentence could easily appear in a blog or a newspaper article. It has a conversational tone and is intended to lead the reader into the rest of the discussion. However, the use of questions and exclamations is regarded as being too informal in academic writing and should usually be avoided.

Note that in places in this book we do use rhetorical devices such as questions. We also write in the first person and address the reader in the second person (you). We have deliberately chosen to write in a more informal style.

One place where many writers do use the first person is in the description of the research process. You will notice this in the article by Webster and Blatchford (2015), for example. Some writers also use it in the introductory sections of an article to explain why they are interested in the topic (see MacClure *et al.*, 2012). Current views about the role of the researcher tend towards the position that the researcher is not a completely 'objective' outsider with no views of their own. This is particularly the case in research using more qualitative methods.

Cautious claims

Another important feature of academic writing in the social sciences is the use of 'cautious language' in making claims to knowledge. This was also discussed in the previous chapter in relation to examining your findings. Examples of cautious language (sometimes referred to as 'hedging') might include sentences containing phrases such as 'this *may* suggest', 'this *could* indicate' or 'this appears to . . . ' Reading language like this can sometimes seem frustrating, especially if we are looking for clear answers. However, most educational research concerns itself with individuals in varied contexts and we cannot predict outcomes with the kind of accuracy that would enable us to talk about 'proof'.

Your research investigation will probably take place *in your* school, with *your* pupils. It would be highly unlikely that the results of your research would be identically replicated in other schools and with other groups of children. However, this does not mean that other people cannot learn from your findings. Using cautious language helps the reader to compare their context with that of your own research and to decide how far they can apply what you have discovered in their own setting.

Below are some verbs and adverbs indicating the range of ways you can discuss your findings and your ideas. These are known as 'modal' verbs and adverbs.

Very confident $\longleftarrow$ $\longrightarrow$ Very cautious

will	may	might	could
definitely	certainly	probably	possibly	perhaps

Be very wary of being over-confident in your claims!

The writer's voice – where do I stand?

While you have been reading research articles you may have noticed that although the writers have used formal academic conventions and avoided the use of emotive language, you will still have a pretty good idea about the opinions many writers hold about the focus and outcomes of their research. Even though they avoid using phrases such as 'I think', we can usually work out what they *do* think from the ways in which the writing is structured and from careful choice of vocabulary. The metaphor that is used to identify this ability is that of 'voice': we are able to 'hear' the writer in their writing.

The use of 'voice' is also an important way to demonstrate 'criticality'. If you have not already read Chapter 4, it would be useful to look at this now and read the section on 'Reading critically' on p48. In this section we discuss the importance of evaluating research claims in the light of the evidence presented. In your writing you need to be able to convey the results of this evaluation in a way that is appropriate within academic writing conventions. This is a subtle art, but it is one that can be consciously developed through the use of certain writing strategies.

Choosing your words

One strategy for developing your critical writing voice involves careful choice of the verbs you might use to introduce ideas from other research. Think of the difference between writing: 'X *asserts* that . . .' compared with 'X has *established* that . . .'

Take note of verbs you have noticed that other writers use in their research writing and reflect on their effect on the reader. This will broaden your own repertoire.

Modal verbs and adverbs (see the previous section) can also be used to express your own views about the claims of other research, as well as your own claims. For example, 'Research by Brown (2010) may *possibly* offer an explanation for . . . '; 'Previous research studies (Smith, 2009; Jones, 2011) *suggest* there *may* be differences . . . '.

Again, try to notice the use of these strategies in your reading and consider their effect, but do remember that some caution about claims is normal in educational research!

Choice of vocabulary can be very important in conveying your opinions (see also the previous extract from Reay (2006) and the commentary in the table at the end of this chapter). Consider what might be the difference between describing something as a 'supposition' rather than an 'interpretation' or even a 'finding'.

The skills of critical reading support your ability to demonstrate criticality in your writing. It would be useful to compile your own lists of verbs, phrases and vocabulary drawn from your reading for later use in your writing.

The referencing issue

Although we said that this chapter would not include detailed information about referencing styles, we do want to emphasise some other important points about the use of academic references in your writing. Technically, the shortened information you provide in the body of your writing is called a *citation*. The full *reference* to the work (title, publisher, place of publication) is provided in a list at the end of the assignment. Providing accurate citations, or references, to indicate the sources of ideas or quotations is not only about avoiding plagiarism, although this is sometimes the main reason given. More importantly, it is also a way of positioning yourself within the academic debate.

As you provide citations to books, articles or other materials you have read, you communicate several things to the reader. You demonstrate your understanding of key ideas in the field through your choice of reading and how you use citation or quotation to support the points you wish to make. You demonstrate how well you are able to evaluate various sources to provide different perspectives. You support your own claims for adding to the existing knowledge about your chosen area by showing how your own work links with that of others, as discussed by Day (2013).

> *acknowledging sources is much more than an annoying convention with which you need to comply. It underpins the very nature of your discipline. The body of knowledge, the practices of the discipline and the people who engage in them are the discipline.*

(Day, 2013, p137)

Conclusion

Academic writing is a recognised type of writing in which a claim to knowledge is presented. This type of writing adheres to conventions that are used to judge the quality of the argument and the claim to knowledge. Most research writing uses a similar structure to ensure coherence in the ways in which claims to knowledge are presented and supported. You need to sequence your writing through clearly connected paragraphs, which enables the reader to understand your overall argument. The use of formal language in academic writing aims at creating a general impression of objectivity in order to develop a convincing argument. While research writing should avoid subjective or over-emotional language, the presence of the researcher within the research is often acknowledged. Your use of academic citation and referencing enables you to demonstrate your understanding of issues and the place of your own research within your chosen area.

Things to think about

1. Is the overall structure of your writing clear so that each section fulfils its intended role?

2. Write out the topic sentences from your paragraphs in each section. Do they represent the key points you are making and a developing argument?

3. Are the points within paragraphs clearly connected? Do paragraphs follow on from one another?

4. Is your language suitably academic?

5. Can you simplify your writing in places?

6. Have you used appropriately tentative language when making claims?

7. Have you checked your referencing carefully?

8. Have you proofread your work?

Commentary on an extract from Reay (2006)

The prevailing *fallacy* for much of the past two decades has been that schools can make all the difference necessary.	Topic sentence of paragraph – main argument. The word *fallacy* is carefully chosen (= a mistaken or false belief).
The school effectiveness and improvement movement was *hegemonic* long enough to have a number of lasting effects (Schostak, 2000).	This sentence presents evidence to support the argument. Again, key vocabulary is carefully selected (*hegemonic* = a dominant idea, usually originating from a powerful group and often unquestioned by others).

(Continued)

(Continued)

The focus was to be on teachers and within school and particularly within classroom processes. If we can only make teachers good enough, equip them with sufficient skills and competencies, then the wider social context of schooling is seen as unimportant. The contemporary 'wisdom' has been that teaching and learning are improved by concentrating almost entirely on concerns about teachers' subject knowledge and pupil performance, both of which are seen to be *de-situated* (Macdonald, 2000).	These sentences <u>explain</u> the assumptions underpinning the 'fallacy' identified in the topic sentence. The use of inverted commas around 'wisdom' implies an opposite meaning. The term *de-situated*, meaning separate from the specific contexts of actual schools and classroom, will form an important link to the argument in the following paragraph.
This has been a *paradoxical* process of, on the one hand, surveillance and prescription in which teachers have been reduced to technicians and divested of much of their earlier scope for autonomy and initiative in relation to pedagogy and curriculum and, on the other, *investing* them with impossible powers of transforming educational failure into success without any of the knowledge and understanding that is necessary before they can even begin to make a small headway into an enormous problem.	This is a long <u>concluding sentence</u>. The writer has deliberately chosen to keep the contrasting ideas in a single sentence in order to emphasise the idea of *paradox* (= a contradictory situation in which both ideas cannot be true). To *invest* someone with powers is to give them control or authority, so the argument is that teachers have simultaneously had their autonomy reduced while being expected to remedy major educational problems.
In contrast, Pat Mahony and Ian Hextall's (2000) insightful analysis shows that the complex relationships and practices inside schools and classrooms require knowledges, approaches and a reflexivity that goes far beyond the skills and competencies approach to teacher training.	The <u>main argument</u> in this paragraph will be 'in contrast' to the ideas outlined previously. The research evidence used links back to, and contrasts with, the word 'de-situated' in the previous paragraph (the complex relationships and practices *inside* schools and classrooms).
Teachers do not simply deliver the National Curriculum and enact a positive discipline policy'; they also confront contextual circumstances such as dilemmas over levels and distribution of resources, acts of violence and aggression, complex patterns of interpersonal and group relationships, power struggles for control and dominance, disputes over achievement, and issues about what constitutes 'really useful knowledge' for different groups of students.	This sentence <u>explains</u> the nature of the 'complex relationships and practices' identified in the topic sentence. By implication it also rejects the 'de-situated' idea of teaching and learning again.
All these multifaceted dilemmas facing teachers are imbued with gender, ethnicity and social class.	A <u>concluding sentence</u> which summarises one of the key arguments of the article.

The paragraph also provides evidence of a strong authorial 'voice'. We are in no doubt about the writer's own views. Words like *fallacy* and *paradoxical* in the first paragraph signal the author's disagreement with some commonly held beliefs about the role of schools in addressing social disadvantage. In the second paragraph, contrasting research is described as *insightful*, and again the prevailing view is rejected in the phrase 'Teachers do not *simply* deliver the National Curriculum'.

References

Day, T (2013) *Success in Academic Writing: Palgrave Study Skills*. Basingstoke: Macmillan.

Gillett, A, Hamond, A and Martala, M (2009) *Successful Academic Writing*. Harlow: Pearson.

MacClure, M, Jones, L Holmes, R and MacRea, C (2012) Becoming a problem: Behaviour and reputation in the early years classroom. *British Educational Research Journal*, 38(3): 447–72.

Reay, D (2006) The zombie stalking English classrooms: Social class and educational inequality. *British Journal of Educational Studies*, 54(3): 288–307.

Webster, R and Blatchford, P (2015) Worlds apart? The nature and quality of the educational experiences of pupils with a statement for special educational needs in mainstream primary schools. *British Educational Research Journal*, V42(2): 324–42.

Further reading

Crème, P and Lea, M (2003) *Writing at University: A Guide for Students* (2nd edn). Buckingham: Open University.

Wallace, M and Wray, A (2006) *Critical Reading and Writing for Postgraduates*. London: SAGE.

Wyse, D (2006) *The Good Writing Guide for Education Students*. London: SAGE

Chapter 9

Looking back and looking forward

Rebecca Austin

Objectives

This chapter:

- summarises the research process;
- asks you to consider the learning that has taken place;
- suggests ways in which your research can be disseminated to others.

In conclusion

You are nearly finished! You have come through a learning process which is now brought to a conclusion – both here and in your project – by drawing together the threads of thinking which have permeated your work. Once you have considered what you have achieved, you can then look ahead to think about how you can share what you have learned with others and where your research, your learning, might take you next.

What have you done?

You have worked through a process of discovery. You started with something that made you curious, which niggled you, which perplexed you or interested you and you set about, systematically, to find out more. What you have learned will stand you in very good stead in your practice when you can say to others: 'I do *this* in the classroom because of what I found out in my research.'

Your written research report can be summarised in the table below. At this point you could think about whether you can you provide a one or two sentence answer to each of the questions.

Introduction	What do I want to find out about and why?
Literature review	What is already known?
Methodology	What is the best way to find it out?
Analysis	What does my data tell me?
Conclusion	What have I found out and why does it matter?

A good research project will have a sense of cohesion. You will feel that there is a strong thread running throughout which clearly identifies what your research is about. The final section, the conclusion, is where you can take a step back and reflect on what you have discovered and the implications for practice for yourself or for others.

What have you learned?

Your conclusion will begin by reiterating what you have found – the answers to the question that you posed at the beginning of your research. We encouraged you to have a narrow focus, so you should be able to provide a focused response. What *is* the effect of hot-seating children as villains in traditional tales on their use of 'voice' in writing? You are highly unlikely to be able to say that you have proved anything or to be able to say that your findings can be replicated and generalised across all schools, all children, all teachers. But what you will be able to say is that you have found out something about whatever it was you set out to discover. Sometimes your key findings are in direct relation to the question you ask and sit comfortably alongside the findings of others which you discussed in your literature review. At other times you might be tentatively challenging findings from different projects and suggesting reasons why your findings should be given due consideration. Sometimes what you have learned has been in relation to research and how best to approach it. You might have learned that children aren't as easy to interview as you had thought or that organising time and space for data collection in a busy primary classroom takes great persistence.

You might have learned something about yourself as a learner. Perhaps you found it harder than you imagined to question or challenge something you believe to be 'right'. You might have found out that your writing skills, your analytical skills and your data-gathering skills were all stretched by the requirements of your project. You might have got to a point where you just had to sit with the data, feeling quite lost and having to trust that the answers would eventually come. This is not a comfortable place to be, but can be the most significant part of the process. It might be that this is significant enough for you to want to write about it in your research report because what you have learned is never just about the question you set out to answer.

What is still to be explored?

The purpose of small-scale research is not to provide answers. In Chapter 2, Judy Durrant described the large-scale randomised control trials which attempt to do that, and suggested that they, too, have their limitations. Small-scale investigations make 'a contribution to knowledge'. You have added something to the mix, but there will be things that you didn't find out – things that were not addressed and things that have emerged from your research which need further investigation.

Your conclusion can include suggestions about where your research might be taken further. If you were working with Key Stage 2 children, would work with Key Stage 1 be interesting? If you used an elicitation approach, is there a way that it could be refined to get more detailed data? If hot-seating had an effect on children's writing, is it worth investigating the best ways to 'do' hot-seating?

You might, too, have had to set aside some potentially interesting findings from your data because you were working to a tight word limit. Was there something to say about gender issues, language use, teacher attitude? These issues and others like them may have been evident in your examination of the data but beyond the focus of your research. These are still potentially interesting to research and can be put forward in your conclusion.

You can also use the conclusion to ponder the puzzles you still have – where answers to your question still seem vague, inconclusive or confusing. You do not need to present a definitive, certain conclusion – as Gill Hope explained in Chapter 5, we are looking at the fuzziness of social life, not the precision of a scientific lens.

Why does it matter?

A significant part of your conclusion is that you are writing about what you have found out and saying why it is important. You need to convince your reader that your findings matter. This still doesn't mean that you need to have found world-changing things – just things that might make teachers think. If your data suggests that boys might like reading stories just as much as they enjoy reading non-fiction, sharing this information with teachers might make them think twice about some assumptions they might be making about the boys in their class. Whatever your findings, they should be a spur to reflection for teachers. If they are uncomfortable with what you have to say, then that might inspire them to undertake research of their own in order to understand it better for themselves.

How will I share my findings?

You now have some findings, something to contribute to the existing understandings of what is already out there. Unless you share what you have discovered with others in some way, your contribution will have very limited impact beyond your own application of your findings to your teaching.

Informally, you can share your findings with others through discussion – other teachers in your school. Perhaps you could offer to lead a staff meeting to talk about what you have found – or you could offer to present as part of a training day with teachers from other local schools?

If your research was part of an assessed piece and you were awarded a distinction or a grade above 70 per cent, you could talk with your tutor about whether and how you could get your work published. A good starting point for publishing practical outcomes from research is through professional magazines or journals. These kinds of publications are designed for teachers who are looking for ideas to implement in the classroom. While you would be referring to literature which supports your suggestions, the focus is more to do with 'how to' do something. For magazines such as these, you would be looking to rewrite your work in a less formal way and present a shorter synopsis of the research which is focused on implications for practice.

More scholarly journals might also be a means by which your research can be disseminated. These sorts of journals will be those that you are likely to have accessed in your study as part of the literature review. Scholarly journals are usually 'peer reviewed' – that is, the article you write is put through a rigorous process of 'checking' before it is published. Submitting articles to peer-reviewed journals often requires some grit and determination, and you need to be prepared to have your work critiqued by experienced others. You are likely to have to review and redraft such articles before they are accepted for publication. While the academic voice you use for scholarly articles will be similar, you will need to adapt the format and the approach to your writing. You will be writing for an audience of your peers, not a marking tutor!

Some universities publish in-house journals which use students' writing and research. It might be worth asking if your institution does this. If they don't, your work might inspire them to start this practice.

An alternative to a solo submission to a peer-reviewed journal is to work with a tutor to produce a jointly authored piece. Your work would form the body of the piece – and this would be acknowledged – but an experienced tutor could prepare the article for submission. You would then be sharing credit for your work but you might be in a better position to get it published.

It could be that your work could be adapted to become a chapter in an edited book. However, unless you know someone who happens to be working on or is interested in producing a book in which your work would fit, this is quite unlikely. Again, you could suggest to someone that a book might be a good idea, especially if you know of other pieces which might complement each other in book form. You could submit a proposal to a publisher yourself, but again this is a competitive and challenging process and you are likely to find it easier if you have someone more experienced who is able to help you with it.

A researchly disposition

Now that you have done one project you must surely have caught the research bug! If you are interested in pursuing further qualifications such as a Master's or doctorate, you could begin by contacting the university where you qualified and see what they have to offer. There are a few pockets of funding available and your head teacher might be willing to fund or part-fund your study, especially if you convince them of the long-term potential benefits to their pupils, their teachers and their school.

While you might not have the idea of pursuing further qualifications just yet, you can still reflect on adopting a 'researchly disposition' that we have talked about throughout this book. The approach I took to buying a popcorn maker which I described in Chapter 1 was that of systematic enquiry. If systematic enquiry seems sensible and right when buying a kitchen appliance, how much more seriously should we take decisions about our teaching? While you will not necessarily engage in rigorous and robust research every time, a researchly disposition means that you think about things more carefully and question why you do things as you do and whether and how they 'work'. This will include engaging in and keeping up to date with the world of research, reading about what others have done, reflecting on their process and their findings, and considering the impact that this might have on your own practice.

You wouldn't be a teacher if you didn't want to make a difference to the lives of the children with whom you work. The biggest and best differences will be seen when you have approached everything you do in the classroom from a thoughtful, researchly and reflective perspective. If someone asks you why you do what you do in the classroom, you want to be able to answer with confidence, knowing that you are answering from an informed and substantiated position.

Further reading

Arthur, J, Waring, M, Coe, R and Hedges, LV (2013) *Research Methods and Methodologies in Education*. London: SAGE.

Aubrey, C, David, T, Godfrey, R and Thompson, L (2000) *Early Childhood Educational Research Issues in Methodology and Ethics*. London: RoutledgeFalmer.

Bell, J (2010) *Doing Your Research Project: A Guide for First-time Researchers in Education and Social Science*. Milton Keynes: Open University Press.

Brown, S, McDowell, L and Race, P (1995) *500 Tips for Research Students*. London: Kogan Page.

Burton, D and Bartlett, S (2005) *Practitioner Research for Teachers*. London: Paul Chapman Publishing.

Burton, N, Brundrett, M and Jones, M (2008) *Doing Your Education Research Project*. London: SAGE.

Clark, A, Flewitt, R, Hammersley, M and Robb, M (2014) *Understanding Research with Children and Young People*. Milton Keynes: Open University Press.

Clough, P and Nutbrown, C (2002) *A Student's Guide to Methodology: Justifying Research*. London: SAGE.

Cohen, L, Manion, L and Morrison, C (2007) *Research Methods in Education*. London: Routledge.

Coles, A and McGrath, J (2010) *Your Education Research Project Handbook*. Harlow: Longman.

Cottrell, S (1999) *The Study Skills Handbook*. London: Palgrave.

Cottrell, S (2005) *Critical Thinking Skills: Developing Effective Analysis and Argument.* London: Palgrave.

Cryer, P (2006) *The Research Student's Guide to Success.* Milton Keynes: Open University Press.

Denscombe, M (2010) *Good Research Guide: For Small-scale Social Research Projects.* Maidenhead: McGraw Hill.

Denzin, NK and Lincoln, Y (eds) (2005) *The Sage Handbook of Qualitative Research.* London: SAGE.

Gee, J (2010) *How to do Discourse Analysis: A Toolkit.* London: Routledge.

Greig, A, Taylor, J and MacKay, T (2012) *Doing Research with Children: A Practical Guide.* London: SAGE.

Hammersley, M (2007) *Educational Research and Evidence-based Practice.* London: SAGE.

Hopkins, D (2002) *A Teacher's Guide to Classroom Research.* Milton Keynes: Open University Press.

Kincheloe, JL (2003) *Teachers as Researchers: Qualitative Inquiry as a Path to Empowerment.* London: RoutledgeFalmer.

Lambert, M (2012) *A Beginner's Guide to Doing Your Education Research Project.* London: SAGE.

Lankshear, C and Knobel, M (2004) *A Handbook for Teacher Research: From Design to Implementation.* Milton Keynes: Open University Press.

McNiff, J (2010) *Action Research for Professional Development: Concise Advice for New and Experienced Researchers.* Dorset: September Books.

Newby, P (2014) *Research Methods for Education.* Harlow: Pearsons.

Opie, C (ed.) (2004) *Doing Educational Research: A Guide to First-time Researchers.* London: SAGE.

Pollard, A (2008) *Reflective Practice: Evidence Informed Professional Practice.* London: Bloomsbury Academic.

Poulson, L and Wallace, M (2004) *Learning to Read Critically in Teaching and Learning.* London: SAGE.

Pring, R (2004) *Evidence-based Practice in Education.* Milton Keynes: Open University Press.

Punch, K (2014) *Introduction to Research Methods in Education.* London: SAGE.

Roberts-Holmes, G (2014) *Doing Your Early Years Research Project.* London: SAGE.

Sharp, J (2009) *Success with your Education Research Project.* Exeter: Learning Matters.

Taber, KS (2007) *Classroom-based Research and Evidence-based Practice: A Guide for Teachers.* London: SAGE.

Taylor, C, Wilkie, M and Baser, J (2006) *Doing Action Research.* London: SAGE.

Thomas, G (2009) *How to do your Research Project.* London: SAGE.

Walford, G (1991) *Doing Educational Research.* London: Routledge.

Wallace, M and Wray, A (2006) *Critical Reading and Writing for Postgraduates.* London: SAGE.

Wilson, E (2009) *School-based Research: A Guide for Education Students.* London: SAGE.

Wyse, D (2006) *The Good Writing Guide for Education Students.* London: SAGE.

Appendix

Format for analysis of a research article

Full reference details of material	Campbell, T (2013) Stratified at seven: In-class ability-grouping and the relative age effect. *British Educational Research Journal* 40(5): 749–71.
What is the <u>main claim</u> made by the author(s)?	In-class ability grouping may adversely affect summer-born children in terms of educational attainment ('mobility') in KS1.
What was the aim of the research and what research methods were used?	The aim was to investigate whether birth–month gradation in teacher perceptions is more pronounced in classes with ability grouping. Statistical analysis of data from the Millennium Cohort study was used. The researcher was not directly involved in designing or collecting the Millennium Cohort study data.
What did the author find out?	The author claims that 'The autumn–summer difference in teacher judgements is significantly more pronounced among in-class ability-grouped pupils than among non-grouped pupils'.
Are the author's conclusions supported by the evidence presented? Could there be other interpretations of this evidence?	The author appears to have considered a number of possible alternative explanations and to have attempted to control for these in different ways.
How does this information relate to my other reading? Are there similarities or differences to other texts I have read?	This is new information, compared to my other reading, but it reinforces the view that ability grouping can be detrimental to the attainment of at least some children.
Does the author make his/her personal viewpoint clear? What is this? How do you know?	The author is opposed to ability grouping in the early primary years. This view appears to be based on the evidence from her analysis of the Millennium Cohort data.
How will I use this information in my literature review?	This research is recent and can be used to support the argument that ability grouping can adversely affect children's progress and attainment in primary schools. I will need to make it clear that this study only looks at the early primary years.

Index